Gaining Perspective

On Pain and Suffering

From Jesus' Healing Touch

*"...To bestow on them
A crown of **beauty instead of ashes**...
They will rebuild...
Restore...and renew
The ancient ruins..."
Isaiah 61:3, 4*

Beauty Instead of Ashes

Susan Groh

SUSAN WARDEN GROH

Order this book online at www.trafford.com/07-0943
or email orders@trafford.com

Most Trafford titles are also available at major online book retailers.

© Copyright 2007 Susan Warden Groh.

All rights reserved. No part of this publication may be reproduced, stored in a retrieval system, or transmitted, in any form or by any means, electronic, mechanical, photocopying, recording, or otherwise, without the written prior permission of the author.

Note for Librarians: A cataloguing record for this book is available from Library and Archives Canada at www.collectionscanada.ca/amicus/index-e.html

Printed in Victoria, BC, Canada.

ISBN: 978-1-4251-2747-3

We at Trafford believe that it is the responsibility of us all, as both individuals and corporations, to make choices that are environmentally and socially sound. You, in turn, are supporting this responsible conduct each time you purchase a Trafford book, or make use of our publishing services. To find out how you are helping, please visit www.trafford.com/responsiblepublishing.html

Our mission is to efficiently provide the world's finest, most comprehensive book publishing service, enabling every author to experience success. To find out how to publish your book, your way, and have it available worldwide, visit us online at www.trafford.com/10510

www.trafford.com

North America & international
toll-free: 1 888 232 4444 (USA & Canada)
phone: 250 383 6864 ♦ fax: 250 383 6804
email: info@trafford.com

The United Kingdom & Europe
phone: +44 (0)1865 722 113 ♦ local rate: 0845 230 9761
facsimile: +44 (0)1865 722 868 ♦ email: info.uk@trafford.com

10 9 8 7 6 5 4 3 2

Contents

Preface and Acknowledgments   5

Introduction   9

Part 1: Snapshots of Jesus

Chapter 1   20
When Joys Runs Out

Chapter 2   30
When Your Bucket Goes Dry

Chapter 3   44
When Hope Withers Away

Chapter 4   58
When Satan Crushes

Chapter 5   74
The Deepest Healing

Chapter 6   88
The Crushing Blow of Accusation

Part 2 : When Life Does Not Make Sense

Chapter 7   99

When God Deliberately Sends Trials

Chapter 8   121

When Heaven is Silent

And Jesus Does Not Answer

Part 3: Personal Reflections

Chapter 9   155

My Personal Journey

Preface

I have had the delightful privilege of serving alongside my husband, Greg, for many years when he was a pastor. Our first church was in Connecticut where we served for nine years. Our second church was in Wisconsin where Greg was a pastor for almost five years, although we stayed in Wisconsin a total of seventeen years. My specific ministries involved teaching the Bible, developing Christian Education, and fostering missions awareness. In my role as pastor's wife, one thing I did not do was counseling. I discovered this when my husband asked me to see a woman with whom he had done some counseling. He thought it would be good for me to see her, to give her godly wisdom from a woman's point of view. I thought it might be a natural fit as well. At our first meeting I listened to her desperate plight and inwardly said to myself, "I do not have the first clue to know what to say that would help!" I thought of scriptures that could relate, but somehow I did not think even they would help. I was really thinking, "You are hopeless, lady!" That hour could not end soon enough. Afterward, I told my husband, very bluntly, "I do not do counseling!" I remembered feeling sad though, thinking it should be natural for a pastor's wife to do counseling. But apparently it was not for me.

When we moved from Connecticut to Wisconsin, God began to change my husband's heart, opening his eyes to the needs in the world. Greg resigned from being a pastor in order to enter the world of global travel, ministering to pastors in many areas of the world. It was a new and exciting challenge for us, which we knew was

Beauty Instead of Ashes

God's will. Greg forged ahead in developing this ministry, while I stayed home to raise the children, traveling with him on occasion. But it was also a time of change for me. God was stretching me and preparing me for another type of ministry, one that I had tried previously, though unsuccessfully. Yes, counseling, but it was different this time. Through circumstances that only God could ordain, I met a delightful and a very godly woman who had a ministry in prisons. She patiently guided me as I counseled with women in prison, leading them to an encounter with Jesus. I learned not to depend on my wisdom, but on God's, and soon I witnessed lives change before my eyes. Finally I was experiencing what genuine counseling can offer, transformation: the effect on a life when Jesus enters, speaks truth, and sets the captive free. It was thrilling to watch as Jesus' encounters with people, recorded in the gospels, became real for the women in prison. Soon I was writing down these experiences, as I realized this was something to be shared with others. It became the basis for this book.

Please allow me to share a few thoughts before we begin. A very important principle with Biblical interpretation is to read the Scriptures literally and naturally as the inspired Word of God. From these we draw applications for life, encouragements in trials, and examples for living. You will notice through my book that I have taken liberty to "fill in some blanks" regarding details of Jesus' encounters. I did so carefully, not to change the original intent, but to bring the Biblical accounts to life. My goal was to stimulate you to think what it would have been like to have been with Jesus. What would you have felt, said, or done? Because the

Preface

Bible does not give all the details that we would like, it leaves us room to ponder some possibilities, like what the people were thinking, or what those who were healed did afterward. I sought to uphold the accuracy and inerrancy of scripture and to heed the warning from scripture to neither add nor delete even a word or letter. My heart's intent was to bring Jesus' life into your own life; for you to experience what common folk did who listened to the Rabbi, or were touched by His hand. They were the ones who experienced true transformation. When they encountered Jesus, they were never the same. For those who were willing to receive, He gave "beauty instead of ashes," a beautiful description from Jesus' mandate for His life, taken from Isaiah 61:3. My prayer is that as you read my book, He will do the same for you!

Acknowledgments

I want to thank several people who are very special to me, and who have given me the courage to press on with this endeavor of publishing. I never set out to write a book, but I realize God has His agenda, and I give Him any praise that may result from this book. I thank and appreciate my husband, Greg, who has been my inspiration for 34 years of married bliss! I love you! I owe so much to my parents, Jim and Betty Warden, for their unfailing love and encouragement to develop into the woman that I am today. I also thank my daughter, Jennifer, who helped to edit the manuscript, and who was a cheerleader throughout. I am deeply grateful to Dr. Nancy Jones, who contributed a wealth of information and wise advice in her thorough editing. My sister-in-law, Debra Warden, designed the delightful front page.

Beauty Instead of Ashes

She has captured the essence of a life that is free from sin and is now clothed in the righteous robes of Christ. Most of all, I am thankful to Jesus for being the answer to the questions of life, and for showing His love and mercy to all in need. Without Him, I would have nothing to write about. This is all about Him.

All scripture references are from the New International Version, unless otherwise noted.

Introduction

God Shows His Love, He Sent Jesus

***God, Are You There;
Jesus, Do You Care?***

Beauty Instead of Ashes

I have read enough and lived long enough to experience what Philip Yancey called, "Disappointment With God." It is that sinking feeling in your gut that stifles a cry of pain born out of deep disappointment with God. The heavens seem too silent, as though God were on vacation and could not care less. It can also be the empty hands that grasp to reclaim what was lost, finding only ashes. Gravesites and memorials reflect memories of what had been but are no more. The fact that heaven holds that which was so precious, so loved, and so needed here seems cruel. I have tried reasoning myself out of this pit and have come alongside others to encourage them, but almost every Bible verse or phrase seems a bit trite and doesn't seem to help at the moment. I am not making light of Scripture. I love the Bible and know it to be the Word of God with all we need for life and godliness. But at times God seems to be up there, somewhere else, and paying attention to others more important than me.

It was at this time that I realized something was not quite right in my own life as I struggled with but could not gain the victory over some personal setbacks and disappointments. I was searching for comfort and relief but mostly for answers to the anguish in my soul. In the midst of depression I remembered thinking, "How could I be depressed, I have so much to be thankful for?" But slowly I realized that most of the inner turmoil was due to being disconnected from God. I wanted to hear Him, to feel His hand of power and comfort, and to know that He truly cared. But it seemed at that moment that He was not there. That emptiness revealed something I had never

Introduction

considered before, that perhaps I was not experiencing God's presence because I had not intimately known His Son, Jesus. Having grown up in a wonderful Christian home, I was familiar with the Bible stories of God. I had accepted Jesus as my Lord and Savior at an early age and I knew of the role of the Holy Spirit. But how well did I really know Them? I realized then that I needed to know Jesus in a new and personal way, to discover that He was truly alive to me. As I went back to re-read the Gospels - personal accounts of those who knew Jesus, lived with Him, and experienced His touch in their lives - I discovered Jesus all over again. I found what my heart was longing for. I finally found His touch on my heart and not just my head. I found peace, hope, and comfort.

There is a need to gain perspective regarding difficult circumstances which threaten our comfort and security and challenge our notion that "God is still on His throne and all is right with the world." It is a perspective Larry Crabb referred to in a talk he gave at Willow Creek Church in Illinois several years ago. He shared an incident that happened to him as a very young boy when he locked himself in his grandparent's bathroom. Suddenly struggling with the terrifying thought, "I'm going to spend the rest of my life in this locked room," he yelled with all his might, "GET ME OUT OF HERE!" His parents quickly surmised his dilemma and leapt into action. His mom, from the other side of the door, comforted and reassured him that help was coming. His father went to the garage to get the ladder, placed it on the side of the house, climbed up and through the window toward the little boy who was struggling to open the door that seemed to mock his vain attempts for freedom. With his dad's ultimate strength, because that's what dads have, he opened the door and triumphantly declared, "You can go out now and play," for isn't that what little boys do?

Years later Larry Crabb received a call from home with bad news of his dad's deteriorating health. In despair and helplessness, Crabb felt himself back as a little boy screaming with all his might, "GET ME OUT OF THIS LOCKED ROOM." Then he envisioned his heavenly Father going to the garage, getting the ladder, setting it against the house, and climbing through the window. But instead of unlocking the door and setting him free to play, God stopped near him. Slowly He sat on the floor and drew Larry into His embrace, whispering in his ear, "It is time to grow up and learn from Me. I can meet all your needs." I believe God desires for each of us to grow up into the realization that life is more than just having the freedom and ability to "play." It is learning of His sufficiency, wisdom, and guidance, often best learned in the midst of the trials of life. It is recognizing that God allows or brings these trials so we can discover that He is all we need as we rest in His embrace. But as we draw near to Him we may discover an aspect of Himself that we did not anticipate.

Throughout Scripture we find God described in majestic but unapproachable terms: Almighty, LORD, transcendent, holy, a burning fire, the Judge, and the Righteous One. Biblical heroes of the faith, like Isaiah, Ezekiel, and John had personally witnessed God in a dramatic manifestation and tried to describe Him. But the best they could do was to describe, using familiar

Introduction

terms, that which was totally unfamiliar to them. The vision of the living God had left them speechless and facedown on the ground. The prophet Isaiah described his vision of God's glory utterly filling the temple and the earth with the heavenly choir of seraphs antiphonally singing His praises. It left him totally undone! Isaiah discovered he could not stand in the presence of the glory of the perfection of God as it revealed his utter sinfulness. Listen as he tries to describe this vision and the effect it had on him.

> *"In the year that King Uzziah died,*
> *I saw the Lord seated on a throne,*
> *High and exalted,*
> *And the train of His robe filled the temple.*
> *Above Him were seraphs, each with six wings…*
> *And they were calling to one another;*
> *'Holy, holy, holy is the LORD Almighty;*
> *The whole earth is full of His glory.'*
> *At the sound of their voices the doorposts and thresholds shook*
> *And the temple was filled with smoke.*
> *'Woe to me!' I cried. 'I am ruined! For I am a man of unclean lips.'"*   Isaiah 6:1-5

One of the best attempts to describe God is Ezekiel's account of a vision he was given during Israel's captivity in Babylon. It was an awesome sight indeed. Listen as he struggles to describe what he experienced.

> *"The heavens were opened and I saw visions of God.*
> *I looked, and I saw a windstorm coming out of the north –*

Beauty Instead of Ashes

An immense cloud with flashing lightning and surrounded by brilliant light.
The center of the fire looked like glowing metal,
and in the fire was what looked like four living creatures.
Spread out above the heads of the living creatures
was what looked like an expanse, sparkling like ice and awesome.
When the creatures moved, I heard the sound of their wings,
like the roar of rushing waters,
like the voice of the Almighty,
like the tumult of an army.
Above the expanse over their heads was what looked like a throne of sapphire,
And high above on the throne was a figure like that of a man.
I saw that from what appeared to be His waist up
He looked like glowing metal,
as if full of fire,
and that from there down He looked like fire;
and brilliant light surrounded Him.
Like the appearance of a rainbow in the clouds on a rainy day,
so was the radiance around Him.
This was the appearance of the likeness of the glory of the LORD.
When I saw it, I fell facedown, and I heard the voice of one speaking."   Ezekiel 1:1b, 4-5a, 22, 24a, 26- 28

Introduction

John in his account of the Revelation describes a heavenly scene filled with the glory of God and the resultant worship that never ends. I am sure it left him speechless and also on the ground.

> *"At once I was in the Spirit,*
> *and there before me was a throne in heaven with Someone sitting on it.*
> *And the One who sat there had the appearance of jasper and carnelian.*
> *A rainbow, resembling an emerald, encircled the throne.*
> *From the throne came flashes of lightning, rumblings and peals of thunder.*
> *Before the throne, seven lamps were blazing.*
> *These are the seven spirits of God.*
> *Also before the throne there was what looked like a sea of glass, clear as crystal.*
> *In the center, around the throne, were four living creatures...*
> *Whenever the living creatures give glory, honor and thanks to Him who sits on the throne and who lives for ever and ever,*
> *the twenty-four elders fall down before Him who sits on the throne, and worship Him who lives for ever and ever. They lay their crowns before the throne and say:*
> *'You are worthy, our Lord and God, to receive glory and honor and power, for You created all things,*
> *and by Your will they were created and have their being.'"*
> *Revelation 4:2-3, 5-6, 9-11*

Beauty Instead of Ashes

Moses, who cried out to know God more, is my favorite Biblical character. Right after the miraculous deliverance out of Egypt, the Israelites had the audacity to rebel and build a cow as a symbol of their God. It was apparent they did not know their God. Moses, however, was given an incredible privilege of knowing God "face to face" (Ex. 33:11), and he pleads with God to spare Israel. God changes His mind and promises that His presence would go with them. But even that was not enough for Moses.

> *"Now show me your glory.*
> *Then the LORD said, 'There is a place near Me where you may stand on a rock.*
> *When My glory passes by, I will put you in the cleft in the rock*
> *and cover you with My hand until I have passed by.*
> *Then I will remove My hand and you will see My back;*
> *but My face must not be seen.'"*
>
> Exodus 33:18, 21-23

Moses yearned for more of God and was not content with just experiencing God from a distance. I believe that pleased God. And in a very real way Moses experienced Jesus, being placed on the Rock and hidden in the cleft of the Rock by God's protective hand. Moses wanted to see God – God showed him Jesus. In His transfiguration in Luke 9: 28-36, not surprisingly Jesus is seen talking with Moses, face to face.

No wonder the Old Testament saints had trouble relating to God. Though they sought to know Him intimately He was veiled in glory and His holiness

Introduction

separated them from Him. Many times God spoke to His people and showed them "signs and wonders," yet many did not experience God in a close and personal way until Jesus came. "In the past God spoke to our forefathers through the prophets at many times and in various ways, but in these last days He has spoken to us by His Son" (Hebrews 1:1-2a). The New Testament completed the Old Testament when it brought God to us in the life of Jesus. God finally showed His love, compassion, and grace to a hurting world. He sent Jesus.

Luke 4:17-21 records the mandate Jesus took for His life, which He read from the scroll of the prophet Isaiah. Though Luke's account is shorter, the Isaiah passage speaks clearly of the ministry He had to so many needy people and the profound effect it had on their lives.

> *"The Spirit of the Sovereign Lord is on Me,*
> *because the Lord has anointed Me to preach good news to the poor.*
> *He has sent Me to bind up the brokenhearted,*
> *to proclaim freedom for the captives and release for the prisoners…*
> *to comfort all who mourn, and provide for those who grieve in Zion…*
> *to bestow on them a crown of beauty instead of ashes,*
> *the oil of gladness instead of mourning,*
> *and a garment of praise instead of a spirit of despair.*
> *They will rebuild the ancient ruins and restore the places long devastated;*
> *they will renew the ruined cities that have been devastated for generations.*

Beauty Instead of Ashes

I delight greatly in the Lord; my soul rejoices in my God.
For He has clothed me with garments of salvation
and arrayed me in a robe of righteousness,
as a bridegroom adorns his head like a priest,
and as a bride adorns herself with her jewels."
Isaiah 61:1-4, 10

In Jesus' three short years of ministry He fulfilled what the scriptures had foretold He would do: preaching the good news, binding up, freeing, comforting, and exchanging joy for sorrow. Israel was an occupied nation whose people were in bondage not only to the Romans but also to the strict traditions and laws of the Pharisees. Jesus saw not only the physical wounds but the emotional and spiritual ones as well. It was to these that He came, to bring wholeness to broken bodies, hope to heavy hearts, and new life to those spiritually lost. More than 2000 years has not changed what He can and wants to do in people's lives.

Do you want to see God, hear from Him, and receive answers to your prayers? He has already done it through Jesus. Jesus said that He came to give life, abundant life. Come with me on a journey to see the God who cares and wants to touch your life with His powerful hand. We will be exploring some familiar stories of Jesus with new insights to ponder and think through. My prayer is that you rediscover Jesus in a new and intimate way, for through this encounter I know that He desires to bestow on you "Beauty Instead of Ashes!"

Part 1

Snapshots of Jesus

His Personal Touch on People's Lives

Chapter One

When Joy Runs Out

When Joy Runs Out

John 2: 1-11 Jesus changes the water to wine at Cana

"On the third day a wedding took place in Cana in Galilee. Jesus' mother was there, and Jesus and His disciples had also been invited to the wedding. When the wine was gone, Jesus' mother said to Him, 'They have no more wine.'

'Dear woman, why do you involve Me?' Jesus replied, 'My time has not yet come.'

His mother said to the servants, 'Do whatever He tells you.'

Nearby stood six stone water jars, the kind used by the Jews for ceremonial washing, each holding from twenty to thirty gallons.

Jesus said to the servants 'Fill the jars with water'; so they filled them to the brim.

Then He told them, 'Now draw some out and take it to the master of the banquet.'

They did so, and the master of the banquet tasted the water that had been turned into wine. He did not realize where it had come from, though the servants who had drawn the water knew. Then he called the bridegroom aside and said, 'Everyone brings out the choice wine first and then the cheaper wine after the guests have had too much to drink; but you have saved the best till now.'

This the first of His miraculous signs Jesus performed in Cana of Galilee. He thus revealed His glory, and His disciples put their faith in Him."

Beauty Instead of Ashes

Weddings in the ancient Near East were the pivotal event of not only one family but of the entire community. The bridegroom would betroth or "engage" his bride-to-be for a time of preparation during which he would do everything necessary to ensure for her a home and security within his father's house. When all was made ready for her, the bridegroom would joyously process through town gathering a crowd of merry friends and neighbors. The long awaited celebration would often last a week. Imagine the delight of the townspeople to hear of a wedding, guaranteeing a banquet and entertainment for all. The bridegroom's family was responsible to provide food and drink for everyone, which would often incur significant debt. Furthermore, if any provision ran out, shame and disgrace would befall them. Such was the dilemma at this particular wedding in Cana in Galilee.

I also love weddings! When our oldest daughter was married there was a whole year of preparation. Although she did the majority of the planning, it was still the overwhelming preoccupation of the entire family. The day finally arrived and I knew it would happen – time started going too fast. I distinctly remember looking around in the church foyer before taking my son's arm to walk down the aisle. Seeing all our family and the friends we had invited, I thought to myself, "This MUST be what heaven is like, surrounded by family and friends and having a glorious celebration. I don't want it to end!"

Don't we long for life to be like that - a long and glorious celebration with family and friends? We enjoy the abundant provisions at a wedding with food that delights and fine wine that makes the heart glad. But at

When Joy Runs Out

this wedding in Cana there was a problem, the wine had run out. This was not a small problem for there were no corner stores to quickly run to and no extra cases of soda to replace the wine. Wine was a staple of life. Diluted wine was normally consumed throughout the day with the best wine reserved for special events. Especially at a wedding the best wine symbolized fullness of life, joy, and prosperity. To run out of wine spelled disaster, not just the disappointment of the guests but an omen of disappointment in life. The bride and groom were toasting to their joyous future and well wishers were drinking to their continuing happiness and success. Wine was the symbol of all they had hoped and dreamed life would be. To run out was unthinkable. But it did.

When I was young, my brother and I used to build our dream houses with Lincoln logs. Remember those wooden, notched beams and inch-long joints that fit together, complete with green plank roofs? But we also fashioned "bombs" out of the joints, putting two jointed pieces together and launching them into each other's buildings by way of a catapult. I remember the joy of working hard, constructing my dream house and pretend horse farm. I also remember the agony of seeing my brother launch his arsenal to destroy my dreams, little by little, so like the reality of life. We all have hopes and dreams for life that are full and rewarding. There is a touching scene in "It's A Wonderful Life" with Jimmy Stewart and Donna Reed. They visit a friend who through hard work and help from the Savings and Loan Bank was able to afford a new house. On the steps to his new house, George and Mary present to this family a basket of bread, a shaker of salt, and a bottle of wine along with this blessing, which interestingly may have originated in the Bible (Psalm 104:15):

Bread – that this house may never know hunger;

Salt – that this house may always have flavor;

Wine – that joy and prosperity may reign forever."

But what happens when you grow up and realize that life is not always like that? What happens when the bombs tear the Lincoln log home apart, when "old man Potter" calls the loan on your home, and when the wine runs out like it did at the wedding in Cana?

Guess who knew when the wine ran out? Mary, Jesus' mother. Aren't moms like that? They know everything. The way she approached Jesus may have revealed her expectation and eagerness concerning the still unannounced true identity of her Son, which she had harbored in her heart for 30 years. You can almost hear her say, "Jesus, You are the Messiah. This is as good a time as any to begin to show Yourself." He replied that His timetable was not quite in line with hers. Nevertheless, she informed the servants to obey whatever He instructed. Somehow she knew He would remedy the situation. Jesus instructed the servants to fill the six stone water jars nearby, the kind used for ceremonial washing. The Jews strictly observed many requirements for ritual and ceremonial cleansing from defilement, many of which required water. Such water was usually kept in common stone or clay jars and was not necessarily clean as it was not used for consumption or food preparation. Whenever someone was aware of the need to be cleansed, water would be scooped out,

When Joy Runs Out

poured, or splashed on the area needing cleansing. It is perplexing that Jesus would command that these common jars be filled. After all, this was a wedding; the problem was the lack of wine. Just imagine how many trips it required the servants to lug buckets from the well in order to fill these jars. There were six jars each holding 20 to 30 gallons. That's a lot of sloshing buckets. The servants might have grumbled under their breath, "What a waste of time. We should be finding more wine." It appeared that Jesus was not meeting the pressing need but was focusing on something totally inconsequential. But a servant did not disobey. Once all the jars were filled, imagine the horror of the servants when Jesus said, "Draw some out and take it to the master of the banquet." Remember, this was water drawn from who knows where. After all, the water in these jars was only for ceremonial use and not for consumption. If you cannot imagine their horror, imagine their amazement when the master of the banquet announced that the bridegroom had kept the best wine till last. What had happened? Provision for the wedding to continue had miraculously been supplied. An abundance of wine had been restored (up to 180 gallons). Joy and gladness would continue with the promise and hope that a full and happy life was still possible. What a happy ending!

How about your life? Did you start out with hopes and dreams of how your life would be? Every child holds in his or her heart countless dreams of a perfect life. Have you noticed how children will pretend to be a teacher, a mother, or a doctor? How many play-act their wedding, dressing even the dog in a frilly dress. Somewhere in the process of growing up those dreams begin to fade in the light of reality. As the dreams burst like bubbles in the breeze, a child's heart begins to harden. Have you seen the hopes and dreams you once treasured in your heart burst or seen them drain away like the empty wine bottles in Cana? Has the joy of life, symbolized by wine, been lacking in your life? Have you experienced the fear of utter ruin when all you had planned and prepared for amounted to nothing? If you answered truthfully, at some time in your life you have experienced what many have: disappointment in life, frustration, and fear when life did not go as planned. Where is God when your dreams vanish and the wine of life's joy drains away? You may have even felt like one of the ceremonial stone jars containing stagnant water, for no special purpose and overlooked as there are other more important containers. If so, Jesus has something to say to you.

Jesus noticed that the wine had run out. He was present at the wedding having been invited to join in the celebration of love. Jesus loves life and delights to celebrate the fullness and joy of life. But like so many celebrations, the unthinkable happened - the source of joy ran out. This celebration was destined to come to a screeching halt and ruin and disgrace were in store for the whole family. But Jesus was there and He was aware. I like to think that it was Mary who prompted Him to act but I believe He would have acted anyway. He is like that. Likewise, how important it is for us to be aware of times when people around us experience the joy draining away, as Mary had noticed the wine running out. We are not to jump in and rescue but we can bring them to Jesus, as Mary did. And together we can watch Him begin to work.

When Joy Runs Out

You see, at some point in the process of turning to Jesus with your need, He begins to fill you. You may wonder why He would bother with someone as insignificant as you when no one else bothered to notice or care. But He notices and He cares and He begins to fill you with His Words, His truths, and His life. It may take time. It will necessitate your cooperation. You may be impatient in waiting and think, "Doesn't He see how great my need is? Why is He taking so long?" But He knows and He continues to fill you. Do not lose patience for in His time He will show you that His filling has changed you. As the water in the jars miraculously became wine, you also will change, but from within. Notice that the stone jars remained the same outwardly. They did not dramatically change into beautiful jars for special occasions. The real change happened inwardly. Jesus can do that for you. In spite of life's disappointments and heartaches, He desires to fill you with Himself. It may not be what you thought at first or how you imagined it would be. You might have initially thought your needs would be met by the things of this world: that money would provide food and clothing, that family would provide love and acceptance, and that jobs would provide security and significance. You may have even looked to God to give you these, thinking they would satisfy your hunger and thirst. It would only be a matter of time before you discovered that the things of this world are shallow and fleeting and people can and will disappoint you. When you realize your needs can never be filled apart from God and you are willing to come to Him, you will see that God desires to give you something different, something infinitely better - His

Beauty Instead of Ashes

Son. The first thing you will discover is your new identity. As Jesus begins to fill you, you will come to understand who you really are - His child, loved and accepted. Once you realize how much He loves you, you will begin to sense your incredible worth and value. You are precious! You are special, to Him! Now you begin to rest in His secure embrace and find the comfort, peace and fullness you had always longed for. Just as more and more buckets of water were needed to fill all the jars, your life can be filled more and more with Jesus. As this process of filling continues you will feel the remarkable touch of Jesus in your life as He changes you. Outwardly you may appear no different, but inward change will be more and more evident as you experience the truth of your new nature, being God's child. And when Jesus fills you with Himself, you can bet it will be the very best!

Do you think the servants continued to look at those stone jars the same way? Of course not. With new respect and profound care they drew from them the wine that Jesus had provided. No longer just ceremonial jars with little significance, these containers were now treated as they really were - jars holding the very best wine. Jesus had looked around for vessels suitable to fill. He saw the jars others had overlooked and knew they would do. For it's not the jar that matters but what fills it. Perhaps those jars continued to provide unlimited wine so the celebration could continue as long as the bridegroom and bride wanted.

How about you? Is there a lack of joy in your life? Do you feel like one of those stone jars, half or mostly empty, and insignificant? In a similar way Jesus is

When Joy Runs Out

looking around and sees you as a jar suitable for filling. Jesus knows what you are going through. He is present and aware that life's dreams may have drained away. His desire is to fill you and to replenish the joy even in the midst of the difficulties in your life. He may not change the outward circumstances, but He will change you inwardly. He wants to fill you with His life so you can enjoy the fullness of life. And He wants you to treat yourself according to the reality of this new life that is in you. Outwardly you may be nothing more than an old stone jar, but with His life in you, you are a special container filled with His source of abundant joy and everlasting life. Because of that, you are worthy of loving care, dignity, and respect. Now you can experience the celebration of a joyous wedding because you are joined to Him in a relationship of love. The disciples were also there and saw this amazing display of His power, the first of His miraculous signs revealing His glory. We read that the disciples put their faith in Him, which was the beginning of their life-changing journey. They discovered the secret to joy - be filled with what Jesus offers, which is Himself. I invite you to also open your heart to receive His filling by His Spirit and experience His joy, without end.

Chapter Two

When Your Bucket

Goes Dry

When Your Bucket Goes Dry

John 4:1-42 The Samaritan Woman

"The Pharisees heard that Jesus was gaining and baptizing more disciples then John, although in fact it was not Jesus who baptized, but His disciples. When the Lord learned of this, He left Judea and went back once more to Galilee.

Now He had to go through Samaria. So He came to a town in Samaria called Sychar, near the plot of ground Jacob had given to his son Joseph. Jacob's well was there, and Jesus, tired as He was from the journey, sat down by the well. It was about the sixth hour.

When a Samaritan woman came to draw water, Jesus said to her, 'Will you give me a drink?' (His disciples had gone into the town to buy food.)

The Samaritan woman said to Him, 'You are a Jew and I am a Samaritan woman. How can You ask me for a drink?' (For Jews do not associate with Samaritans.)

Jesus answered her, 'If you knew the gift of God and who it is that asks you for a drink, you would have asked Him and He would have given you living water.'

'Sir,' the woman said, 'you have nothing to draw with and the well is deep. Where can you get this living water? Are you greater than our father Jacob, who gave us the well and drank from it himself, as did also his sons and his flocks and herds?'

Jesus answered, 'Everyone who drinks this water will be thirsty again, but whoever drinks the water I give him will never thirst. Indeed, the water I give him will become in him a spring of water welling up to eternal life.'

The woman said to Him, 'Sir, give me this water so that I won't get thirsty and have to keep coming here to draw water.'

Beauty Instead of Ashes

He told her, 'Go, call your husband and come back.'

'I have no husband,' she replied.

Jesus said to her, 'You are right when you say you have no husband. The fact is, you have had five husbands, and the man you now have is not your husband. What you have just said is quite true.'

'Sir,' the woman said, 'I can see that you are a prophet. Our fathers worshiped on this mountain, but you Jews claim that the place where we must worship is in Jerusalem.'

Jesus declared, 'Believe Me, woman, a time is coming when you will worship the Father neither on this mountain nor in Jerusalem. You Samaritans worship what you do not know; we worship what we do know, for salvation is from the Jews. Yet a time is coming and has now come when the true worshipers will worship the Father in spirit and truth, for they are the kind of worshipers the Father seeks. God is Spirit, and His worshipers must worship in spirit and in truth.'

The woman said, 'I know that Messiah' (called Christ) 'is coming. When He comes, He will explain everything to us.'

Then Jesus declared, 'I who speak to you am He.'

Just then His disciples returned and were surprised to find Him talking with a woman. But no one asked, 'What do you want?' or 'Why are you talking with her?'

Then, leaving her water jar, the woman went back to the town and said to the people, 'Come see a man who told me everything I ever did. Could this be the Christ?' They came out of the town and made their way toward Him.

Meanwhile His disciples urged Him, 'Rabbi, eat something.'

But He said to them, 'I have food to eat that you know nothing about.'

When Your Bucket Goes Dry

Then His disciples said to each other, 'Could someone have brought Him food?'

'My food,' said Jesus, 'is to do the will of Him who sent Me and to finish His work. Do you not say, "Four months more and then the harvest?" I tell you, open your eyes and look at the fields! They are ripe for harvest. Even now the reaper draws his wages, even now he harvests the crop for eternal life, so that the sower and the reaper may be glad together. Thus the saying "One sows and another reaps" is true. I sent you to reap what you have not worked for. Others have done the hard work, and you have reaped the benefits of their labor.'

Many of the Samaritans from that town believed in Him because of the woman's testimony, 'He told me everything I ever did.' So when the Samaritans came to Him, they urged Him to stay with them, and He stayed two days. And because of His words many more became believers.

They said to the woman, 'We no longer believe just because of what you said; now we have heard for ourselves, and we know that this man really is the Savior of the world.'"

Beauty Instead of Ashes

Jesus and His disciples set out on a journey. Their plan was to leave Judea in order to minister in Galilee. As was the custom of all good Jews, they would bypass Samaria. Historically, Samaria was the capital of the northern kingdom of Israel, which was conquered by Assyria in 723 BC. The best of the population was deported to Assyria while foreigners were imported to mix with the remaining poor and introduce pagan religions opposed to Judaism. It was the conqueror's way of ensuring submission and of breaking their spirit and will. From that time on the Jews of Judea looked with distain on Samaria, treating Samaritans as heretics and calling them mixed-breeds or "dogs." In their contempt, the Jews even barred the Samaritan's access to the temple in Jerusalem, virtually condemning them to the status of a Gentile or an unbeliever. Without the ability to offer sacrifices in Jerusalem, salvation was impossible. Having no choice, the Samaritans constructed their own temple for worship. As a result the Jews added "idol worshiper" to their condemnation of the Samaritans. The Samaritans returned insult and injury as they were able and the animosity brewed. Isolation and avoidance became the norm. It was for this reason that the Jews went around Samaria whenever traveling from Judea to Galilee. (Knowing this history, can you imagine the audible gasps from the religious Jews when Jesus shared His not-so-subtle story "Who is my neighbor" featuring the Samaritan as the "good neighbor?" Undoubtedly, Jesus' story created tension!)

Notice what the text says in John 4:4, "Now He had to go through Samaria." No typo, this was a divine appointment. As the small band of followers crossed the

When Your Bucket Goes Dry

boundary of Judea into Samaria, Jesus' steps were sure and confident. The disciples however, must have struggled inwardly, wondering where this Rabbi was taking them. After a while, Jesus, being tired from the journey, sat down by a well. He knew what it was like to be hot and thirsty. He knew someone else was going to be there, a certain woman who was also hot, tired, and thirsty.

This story reminds me of summers in upstate New York. Everyone looks forward to the summer's warmth after the winter's icy blast. On long summer days I work alongside my mother in the garden or help my brother cut down trees and stack firewood for the winter, which always seems to come too soon. There is never an end to the chores that need tending: weeds to be pulled, lawns to be mowed or windows to be cleaned. At the end of a hot summer's day I look forward to jumping in our pool and drinking a tall glass of iced tea. But what if there were no pool, no iced tea, and no escape from the heat? Though it tends to be hot in New York in the summer, it is even hotter in Israel. Having visited Israel in the summer, I learned first hand of the oppressive heat in the Middle East. It is so overpowering that it forces you to seek relief in any oasis where there is shade and water. When Jesus sat down by the well, He had no means by which to draw water from the well to satisfy His thirst. He was legitimately thirsty, experiencing a real need. He also had a plan. Sure enough, along came the Samaritan woman with the means to quench His thirst, her bucket. But why in the world was she drawing water from the well at that time of day? After all, it was the sixth hour or about twelve, noon. We need to read between the lines to see what was really going on.

We learn from Jesus' interaction that she had been married five times and presently was living with a man out of wedlock. There are a number of possible explanations for this woman's plight. Keep in mind that this was a male dominated culture and a woman had few rights. The man had the right to divorce, not the woman. One consideration is that she might have been barren, unable to bear children. In the Hebrew culture this would have been tantamount to disaster. By not fulfilling her primary role of bearing children, the family line would end. Without children there was no guarantee of social security, for children would ensure their parents' elderly care. Without children there would be no preservation of the family land. Moses allowed the people to divorce on these grounds and it was all too common. Being divorced, she would not have had the financial security provided by a husband. Women in such situations could turn to prostitution or return to their family. Either way she would be branded as useless, even cursed by God for not fulfilling her role of bearing children. If this were the case, perhaps she kept trying to conceive with different husbands but with the same sad results: a dry and empty womb and no security for her future.

Try to imagine how she felt; she had so much going against her. She was a poor woman in a male dominated society and despised because she was a Samaritan. Perhaps, because she was barren, she was divorced many times. Now she was shunned because she was living

When Your Bucket Goes Dry

with a man who apparently was content to use her but to give her no dignity through marriage. She was forced to draw water in the heat of the day to avoid being embarrassed by other women of stature. Perhaps they communicated in very clear ways that "her kind" was not welcome in the cool of the early morning or evening, when other respectable women would be drawing water for their families. After all, their fruitfulness must be evidence of God's love and blessing. Therefore, their scorn for this woman was justified and so she bore her shame as an outcast. Adding to her despair was the demand of having to continually refill her bucket. Its emptiness discouraged her as it reminded her of her empty soul, which also could never find fulfillment. Day after day she endured the long, lonely journey to the well, alone.

Have you ever been to this well, holding your empty bucket, and wondering if life would ever be full and satisfying again? In the popular musical, Les Miserable, the tragic figure Fantine sings a heart-rending song of despair, "I Dreamed a Dream":

There was a time when men were kind.
When their voices were soft
And their words inviting.
There was a time when love was blind
And the world was a song
And the song was exciting.
There was a time.
Then it all went wrong.

Beauty Instead of Ashes

I dreamed a dream in time gone by
When hope was high
And life worth living.
I dreamed that love would never die
I dreamed that God would be forgiving.
Then I was young and unafraid
And dreams were made and used and wasted.
There was no ransom to be paid
No song unsung
No wine untasted.

But the tigers come at night
With their voices soft as thunder
As they tear your hope apart
As they turn your dream to shame.

He slept a summer by my side
He filled my days
With endless wonder.
He took my childhood in his stride
But he was gone when autumn came.
And still I dream he'll come to me
That we will live the years together.
But there are dreams that cannot be
And there are storms
We cannot weather.

I had a dream my life would be
So different from this hell I'm living.
So different now from what it seemed.

When Your Bucket Goes Dry

Now life has killed
The dream I dreamed.
(Permission pending from Alain Boublil Music Ltd.)

Being left with a child, on the brink of despair with nowhere to turn, Fantine gives up hope. Yet there was one who did turn aside to consider her plight, took pity on her, and reached out to offer hope. Jean Valjean raises Fantine's child after her untimely death. Though it was too late for Fantine, it was not too late for this woman of Samaria.

Try to picture Jesus sitting at the well, shading His eyes with His hand, and watching the solitary figure slowly walking toward Him. The bucket she carried, though empty, seemed heavier with every step. Her eyes were downcast and her steps were slow. She had nothing important to do really: no little babies at home, no small son to help carry the bucket, and no respectable husband for whom to prepare dinner. Life was cruel. Life had killed the dream she had once dreamed. As she approached the well Jesus spoke to her, "Will you give me a drink?" Dumbfounded, she must have stumbled back on her heels, her mind reeling as she grasped the reality, "He spoke to me! Jews do not speak to such as me!" Yet He did and she would never be the same. You see, Jesus conferred dignity on this poor woman who was not just ignored but snubbed, even by her own people. He did this first by speaking to her, acknowledging her presence. How many times do we avoid eye contact with a stranger, passing them by without even a nod of the head? It is this kind of treatment which shrivels the spirit, diminishing the worth of a person. Jesus not only spoke to her but He asked her for a drink, revealing His need for something she could provide. Though it seemed small and insignificant, by asking for her help He met one of the most important basic needs that all people have: to feel valued and to have a sense of worth. She had a bucket, He had a need. If she chose to, she could meet His need and literally save His life in the desert. As He continued talking with her, He revealed that He had something to give her, which He described as living water. You can imagine her interest: no longer having to go to the well in the heat of the day, drawing water with an incessantly empty bucket, and being reminded of the emptiness of her own life. Instead she could have living water, ever flowing, never-ending, fresh and abundant! How good it must have sounded, appealing to her dry, empty soul and weary feet. Who wouldn't want this living water? But first she had to acknowledge the truth of the emptiness of her soul. Jesus commanded, "Go, call your husband." What a cruel request, especially since He knew her condition. Did she wince? Perhaps, so she gave a guarded reply in an attempt to hide the pain in her soul. I am reminded that the most well known organization that deals with addictions makes it mandatory for group members to admit guilt each time they gather together. Alcoholics Anonymous knows that the only way to begin healing is by admitting the truth; "I am weak and in need of help." Jesus wanted this woman to stop fighting, to stop avoiding the truth, and to admit her guilt and acknowledge the emptiness of her soul. He wanted her to call out to Him for help. That is why He was there. It was because He loved her that He revealed His power to know her so deeply and so well. When frightened by His insight she correctly surmised, "I can see that You are a prophet!" Have you ever been under the spotlight of God's eyes? It is no fun to squirm, looking for a hiding place as His penetrating light reveals all the ugly, sordid truths of your life. She deflected His inquiry with accusations of how the Jews had oppressed the Samaritans. "Look what you Jews have done. It's not our fault!" Then He gently shifted the conversation to what was really important, who He was, the Messiah. How I would have loved to have been there, to watch her face change from despair to bewilderment to overwhelming shock of Who was talking with her!

Interruptions – don't you hate interruptions? But I think Jesus allowed, even ordained for the disciples to return at that time from their trip to get food. The woman needed to be able to compose herself and think through what had just happened. As the truth of Jesus' Words took hold in her empty heart, she did the only thing that made sense - she dropped her bucket! Did her circumstances change? Did He heal her barrenness? Did He command the man she lived with to marry her, giving her security and dignity? No. Then what did He do that made such a difference? Jesus met her most basic needs for love and acceptance, value, and worth. He loved her by spending time with her and treating her as a woman of worth, not based on what she did but who she was. He patiently corrected her understanding of the real truth regarding her nationality and even true worship. He included her in His plan by showing her a purpose for living - sharing the good news of the coming of the Messiah. Loved, accepted, secure, and significant, she

Beauty Instead of Ashes

dropped her bucket! She did not need it anymore. She was no longer thirsty. She had met the Savior and her response gave evidence that she was now a child of God. Imagine the change on her face, for she was now complete. This barren woman was now filled with joy. The living water the Messiah had told her of now poured into her heart, quenching her thirst for life and meaning. It made a profound difference. This woman met the Messiah and found new respect and dignity, which enabled her to become the town's first evangelist. Jesus commissioned her and her life produced fruit.

How about your life? Are you experiencing hunger or thirst? Is your soul dry and withered? Have you looked for love, sought worth, or pursued significance? Life can be so very mundane, chores and duties demand attention and so little is given back. Respect and dignity are cherished commodities, but you may not be experiencing them due to your own failures or the failures of others. Does God care? He showed His care for this woman. Will you believe that He cares for you? The Samaritan was doubtful and had good reason, so God sent Jesus to her. He does the same for you. Jesus is standing next to you. Oh, you don't hear Him, not audibly, but through the eyes of faith you can hear Him say to you what He said to the woman by the well; "Do you want what I have? I will give you living water for your thirsty soul. I will give you significance to realize who you are and what I can do through you. Will you allow My Holy Spirit to fill your soul so you can finally and forever leave your bucket behind? Now go into the world with your head held high, for you go for Me."

When Your Bucket Goes Dry

It is time to drop your bucket. In Jesus' day to do so was suicide for a bucket was a lifeline to water, which was life itself. It was probably scary for the woman to consider, "If I drop it, I may never find it. Someone else will snatch it up. Then I will surely die. But if I don't drop it, I will miss what this new life is all about." Maybe in her confusion and fear she looked again to this Man. The disciples were approaching. She was probably thinking, "Would He be focusing on them now? After all, they are much more important than I am." But I think He was still watching her. Eye to eye, He continued to affirm the truth of what was slowly dawning on her. He was already filling her with living water. He must have smiled when she smiled, for she let go of her bucket. It's time to drop your bucket, too. Trust Jesus, He is looking at you, ready to fill you. Let Him do to you what He did to the Samaritan woman.

Chapter Three

When Hope

Withers Away

When Hope Withers Away

John 5:1-15 Healing the Invalid by the Pool

"Some time later, Jesus went up to Jerusalem for a feast of the Jews. Now there is in Jerusalem near the Sheep Gate a pool, which in Aramaic is called Bethesda and which is surrounded by five covered colonnades. Here a great number of disabled people used to lay – the blind, the lame, and the paralyzed. One who was there had been an invalid for thirty-eight years. When Jesus saw him lying there and learned that he had been in this condition for a long time, He asked him, 'Do you want to get well?'

'Sir,' the invalid replied, 'I have no one to help me into the pool when the water is stirred. While I am trying to get in, someone else goes down ahead of me.'

Then Jesus said to him, 'Get up! Pick up your mat and walk.'

At once the man was cured; he picked up his mat and walked.
The day on which this took place was a Sabbath, and so the Jews said to the man who had been healed, 'It is the Sabbath; the law forbids you to carry your mat.'

But he replied, 'The man who made me well said to me, "Pick up your mat and walk."'

So they asked him, 'Who is this fellow who told you to pick it up and walk?'

The man who was healed had no idea who it was, for Jesus had slipped away into the crowd that was there.

Later Jesus found him at the temple and said to him, 'See, you are well again. Stop sinning or something worse may happen to you.' The man went away and told the Jews that it was Jesus who had made him well."

Beauty Instead of Ashes

Our country endured the fury and aftermath of Hurricane Katrina, a category four hurricane in the summer of 2005. It hit Louisiana and Mississippi with a vengeance, swamping low-lying New Orleans with devastation and misery. New Orleans was once the jewel of the South where fabled parties celebrated life, fun, and happiness amid historically beautiful streets and boulevards. Instead, we witnessed endless pictures of tens of thousands of people wading through polluted water having lost everything. Huddled together many refugees sought relief in the Superdome, only to endure blistering heat, humidity, and indescribable stench. As helicopters and trucks tried to deliver relief supplies, many crowds rioted to obtain such basics as water and food. People were literally dying in the open as supplies could not reach them fast enough. A question like, "Do you want help?" would have deserved a slap in the face or received a mournful, pitiful cry. Jesus asked such a question in the midst of a very similar scene set two thousand years ago.

Try to imagine a shallow pool filled with refuse whose banks were littered with crippled and broken bodies. The area was not large where so many had lain, where open sores oozed pus onto the muddy banks and into the warm dank water. How many had literally died there, their corpses beginning to rot? Oppressive heat and humidity compounded inhumane conditions and squalor. Many had come hoping for a cure, a last-ditch effort in a lifetime of dashed hopes. A rumor had it that once a year an angel came down, stirred the water, and the first one in the troubled water was cured. Whether this rumor was true no one can be sure but for those

When Hope Withers Away

huddled around the pool, eyes intent on seeing that first faint ripple, it was real - it just had to be! Now imagine as a faint hint of breeze ripples the water, causing instant panic. Desperate people kicking and clawing to get into the water, fighting, and straining to pull others out of the way in order to be the first to flop into the polluted pool. I wonder if any had been cured, if any had walked out whole and healed. Yet hope fueled by desperation does not give up easily. It was into such a scene that Jesus walked and looked around. Was He looking for someone in particular? Jesus saw a man and inquired about him. Apparently, He had a plan. Thirty-eight years was a long time for anyone to wait for an answer to prayer, for a miracle. Jesus made His move, approached the man, and asked a simple question, "Do you want to get well?" One has to wonder if the question needed to be asked considering the situation. The man answered; "I have no one to help me into the pool." True enough or perhaps was it an excuse? Had he lost hope many years ago? Might he have uttered under his breath, softly cursing those who spoke of a loving God and a tender Savior? "Rubbish! Not for me!" His hope now lay in the possibility of someone helping him into the water. But after so many years of trying, waiting, and failing, was he fooling himself? Maybe that's why he did not recognize Jesus; he was still intently looking at the water. Some might think Jesus was cruel to ask the question, a sort of morbid reminder of the invalid's miserable state. We also have no way of hearing the man's tone of voice. Was it pitiful, pained, angry, bitter, or remorseful? What would you have felt, I wonder? What would you have answered?

Beauty Instead of Ashes

Waiting no longer, Jesus' strong voice was heard; "Get up! Pick up your mat and walk." The time for waiting was over. There was no more need to watch for the wind to stir the polluted waters where healing might take place. Jesus' healing power flowed into this empty shell of a man. What might he have felt? Perhaps he experienced a shock wave coursing through his broken body or perhaps just a tingling sensation flowing down into his lifeless legs and feet? It was a miracle how muscles and ligaments that had not worked for 38 years now hoisted him to his feet. This cruel crippling was reversed in an instant! Awkwardly and hesitantly he moved away from the pool's edge. Slowly yet confidently he left behind a living death and entered the world of the healthy and whole, walking as if he was flying, finally free. God had heard his cry.

Let's look a bit closer. In verse three it says that the man was "disabled," literally "not able." We have no way of knowing how he got in that condition but have you ever felt like this man? Have you ever felt unable, inferior, and useless? Have you thought, "What's the use, I can't, never could?" Words like these become labels that generate pain and suck the hope out of you. This man had all but lost his hope to get well. So how did Jesus know him and why did He choose to heal him? We will never know but we can take comfort in knowing that Jesus knew and loved this man despite his state of hopelessness. Can you put yourself in his place and begin to believe that Jesus sees you right now and loves you, too? Jesus showed His power to heal even this man - one whom most had said was beyond hope. Truly, nothing is impossible with God! And though Jesus is

When Hope Withers Away

fully capable of healing both physical and emotional disabilities, it is true that some who suffer in this lifetime may not be completely healed, despite their faith in Him. Nevertheless, His words are still spoken for He desires to free you from perhaps something far worse than physical crippling. You may be struggling with an inward, emotional crippling that keeps you "disabled," with seemingly no one to rescue you or bring you healing. It may seem like this has gone on for many years and that your life has been a cruel waste. If this is so, I want you to consider that what Jesus said to this man He says to you as well. Jesus' healing of this man was more than just physical; the deeper healing was in his soul. We look at the healthy body as the greatest prize but Jesus sees the inward soul as having much more importance. When Jesus healed this man physically, He did so in order to bring complete healing, more than this man knew he needed. Like this man who did not recognize Jesus, you may not recognize that Jesus is right beside you, asking if you want to be healed and made well again. What answer will you give Him? Will you make excuses for why you are not living the way God intended? Or will you show in your attitude and your actions that you have lost hope long ago? Nevertheless, Jesus is speaking to you and telling you to "Get up! Pick up your mat and walk!" This is a command from Jesus, which you can obey, too. He would not tell you to do something you could not do. Jesus offers you healing from despair and every other belief that devastates you so that you can experience a renewed spirit, encouragement, and peace. Jesus can sustain you through even the most difficult circumstances. By trusting Him you can experience abundant life, despite infirmities and limitations. His power is absolute and when He gives a command even the angels and demons shudder! Will you trust Him and begin to move toward life? This man did not know of Jesus' power till he literally began to straighten his lifeless legs and found he could. Then he put those skinny legs underneath his shriveled body, began to push himself up and found he could. You can do the same right now. Start to move toward emotional healing, believing the power to do so is God's will. No matter what crippling belief holds you in bondage, you can be free! When Jesus looks at you He does not look at your outward condition but your inward heart. He sees your pain and the effect it has in breaking and crippling you. But Jesus comes near and speaks to you these same words, "Get up, come alive, and be restored!" Hearing His Words and responding by faith, you can move toward hope and healing. Crippling comes in many forms. You may be physically crippled, but Jesus still beckons, "Get up!" You may be trapped in an oppressive situation, home, marriage, job, or even a country where your freedoms are taken away, but Jesus still urges, "Get up!" You may be emotionally crippled, holding onto anger and bitterness because of abuse or neglect. Jesus still says to you, "Get up!" Circumstances which trap you and cripple you tend also to blind you to the truth that Jesus is near, He did not leave. Like the man Jesus spoke with, if you focus only on the hurt and pain, you too may see no hope and eventually give up. You may even become that which cripples you; it is now your identity. But Jesus came into the world to save you and free you from the crippling effect of sin and the bondage of lies.

When Hope Withers Away

By refocusing your eyes on Him you can experience hope. He may not reverse the physical crippling but He will give you the ability to overcome any emotional or spiritual barrier, if you trust Him. Let's continue to discover what His commands will entail.

"Pick up your mat!" It was a strange command. I have pondered it for some time. Frankly, I would have left it behind. Why carry a reminder like that when you can finally be free? That stinking mat represented years of agony, sorrow, bitterness and tears, and a crushing judgment of being "unclean" in the Jewish culture. Jesus knew that and because He wanted this man's healing to be complete, He carefully instructed him what to do. "Walk!" Walk where? Away from the pool, first of all! I would think the man would not need encouragement, but would have run. So where did he walk? He went into the temple where ironically, he was accused of doing "work" on the Sabbath, carrying his mat. Nevertheless, it was where he needed to go. Presenting oneself to a priest after being healed from a defiling illness was a normal part of Jewish life (Luke 17:14). To display the evidence of healing was to ensure the pronouncement of cleansing and therefore the ability to re-enter Jewish life. This man's mat was evidence enough of his miserable state of being unclean but the fact that he walked into the temple, carrying his mat, showed undeniable proof of a miracle. The priest should have joyfully pronounced, "You are clean" and then disposed of the mat, once and for all separating the man from the evidence and reminder of his years of bondage. By leaving the mat at the temple, the man would have completed his healing, both outwardly and inwardly.

Beauty Instead of Ashes

To bring the mat to the priest is similar to what Jesus now commands us, "Give all your worries and cares to God, for He cares about what happens to you" (1 Peter 5:7 New Living Translation). Jesus is asking us to bring Him all our pain, sorrow, agony, bitterness, and tears. These are the things that so often cripple us, that keep us from living the full and free life God intends. They have become that stinking, rotting mat we find ourselves lying on. But when we bring them to the cross, Jesus takes them from us, freeing us, and enabling the healing to begin. Doctors and counselors often encourage wounded people to "embrace the pain," knowing it is part of the healing process. To be gut-wrenchingly honest about pain is to deal with the reality surrounding it and resolve the painful issues connected to it by doing the hard work of forgiving, seeking restoration, reclaiming the truth, putting the past behind, and entering the future. Only then, can one be truly healed and restored.

Jesus knew that when He asked the man to "pick up your mat," He would find him at the temple. The true healing had just begun. Just consider the processing this man did as he picked up that loathsome mat and carried it away from the pool of despair. A pronouncement by the priest, "You are clean" was dependent on what the man was willing to do with all that the mat represented. Ultimately, the man would leave the temple, but would he still be carrying his mat? How many people still do? Physically it was repulsive, stinking and rotting. It was graphic evidence of many years of suffering. The same applies to us. Jesus wants total healing, which includes the inner healing, often more crippling than physical illness. When we consider what our "mat" represents, we

When Hope Withers Away

are ready for Jesus to show us how to bring it to Him to begin our healing. He wants to pronounce, "You are clean!" It is dependent on what we are willing to do. For too long this man felt helpless as he sat by those waters, which could never cleanse him. Are we also waiting?

Pain is a funny thing. Do we sometimes get comfortable in our pain? Initially we fight against it with all our might. We pray like never before, beseeching God to take it away. God, who is all-knowing, may allow pain for our good. Peter, Jesus' disciple, shared what he learned through trials in 1 Peter 5:6, "Humble yourselves, therefore, under God's mighty hand, that He may lift you up in due time." Most of the time we experience God's wonderfully protective hands which hold us so securely, as illustrated in John 10: 28, 29: "I give them eternal life, and they shall never perish; no one can snatch them out of My hand. My Father, who has given them to Me, is greater than all; no one can snatch them out of My Father's hand." But sometimes those hands appear to slip out from under us and we panic. We don't feel those solid, strong hands underneath anymore. Now His hand seems to be pressing down on us with a weight and force that seems unbearable. We shout in our pain and confusion, "What is happening? Where is God? What about those precious promises we memorized as children so long ago?"

Little do we realize or like to remember that Scripture speaks of the refiner whose job it is to purify silver (Zechariah 13:9, Malachi 3:3). The refiner knows how to do it best – with fire. He prepares the fire, places the lump of silver in a container, and lets the fire do its job of drawing the impurities out the hotter it gets. As the impurities rise to the top he skims them off but keeps the heat up. Can you guess when he knows it is pure? When he can see his face reflected in the surface of the silver. The Refiner of our lives is God who knows what is needed in order to purify us, to free us from what pollutes and ruins us. 1 Peter 5: 6 says, "Humble yourself under God's mighty hand, until He lifts you up." Easy to say when things are going well. But in the heat of the moment we tend to squirm out from under the trial of His mighty hand, push against the pressure, maneuver, manipulate, bargain, and, at our wits end, cry out in despair for help or relief. Still He exerts the pressure, for He knows the result will be worth it. He loves us that much. Funny how wise Scripture is, "Humble yourself." If we did that to begin with, trusting that our Heavenly Father knows what is best, the trial of fire would have been much briefer. His work of skimming off our wrong beliefs, harmful behaviors, illegitimate dependencies, and unbecoming characteristics would have produced the desired results - purity. When we begin to reflect the beauty of Jesus in unwavering trust, willing obedience, and selfless love, we will experience Him lifting us up, revealing that the painful refining was part of His will. This is hard to contemplate - that God uses pain, in fact sometimes brings pain, but it is always for our good. I believe that when we recognize God's loving hand at work in the trial, then we can trust Him, no matter what He allows in our lives. Will you consider how God may be active in your pain to produce in you a refining of your character?

When Hope Withers Away

What happens when we won't humble ourselves or submit to God's refining? Too often we suffer needlessly as we fight God's heavy hand of purifying. Instead of becoming refined we become hard, bitter, and withdrawn. Soon even our understanding and perception is clouded and we forget why God might be doing this. We may even think that God is against us. Trials often produce volatile emotions such as anger and bitterness. If these emotions are not dealt with or resolved but are turned inward, they will simmer and grow until they begin to mask the truth. We then mistakenly believe the falsehood that God is cruel and unfair. The growing emotional pain seems to threaten our very lives, like angry storm clouds that build on the horizon and threaten to obliterate the sun. It doesn't stop there. When joy and life are blotted out the spirit shrivels, becoming like a cripple, and we are no longer able to enjoy relationships with loved ones and friends. Commiserating with similar sad victims provides an escape. "At least they understand" we sadly say and we tend to stay with them, keeping our bandages wound tightly and the crutches nearby. Was this the sad tale of the man Jesus found by the pool? When Jesus healed him, He told him to walk. It was time to leave the pool, his past, and all that identified him as a cripple. There was work to be done.

Once at the temple Jesus greeted him. The man might have just finished presenting himself and the mat to the Priest and received a pronouncement of cleansing. But Jesus knew there was even further need of healing, a cleansing of his soul. "See, you are well again. Stop sinning or something worse may happen to you!" I am disappointed that we cannot see the man's facial features or body language when Jesus spoke to him. Was he indignant to such a remark, cut to the quick and insulted? Or was he grateful for his healing and quick to take to heart this further admonishment, which possibly regarded his future and eternal security? When Jesus said "well again," and "stop sinning," He seemed to be inferring that the man's condition was a result of prior sin. Perhaps his years of suffering were intended to bring him to a place of repentance. Jesus now warned of something worse if he persisted in sin. Certainly the man could think of nothing worse than going back to that pool again as an invalid. Or, was Jesus talking about leaving his sinful state through repentance, so as to not find himself in hell? Either way we can be sure that Jesus informed him and us, that if we don't do something about our sin now, we may see more pain and suffering in this life and something infinitely worse after death. We do not know if this man was born crippled, became crippled due to sin, or experienced the natural consequences of living in a fallen world where sometimes bad things happen to good people. We do know that Jesus wanted him to be sure of his future, so He came to him and presented another option. Through repentance this man could avoid something worse than the "pool of despair."

The same applies for you and me. If you can identify with this man in his horrible physical condition and you feel that your hope is ebbing away, take heart. Although Jesus may not heal your body, He offers healing for your soul and an eternity of wholeness and joy when you step out of this temporary dwelling and

When Hope Withers Away

into heaven's never ending bliss. If you are not in an agonizing situation right now, let this be a wake-up call for you; life on earth is not eternal. What you do now will determine your eternal destiny. Jesus offers you eternal life through forgiveness of sins through His death on the cross. It is for you, dependent on repentance ("stop sinning") and obedience to His Word. I urge you, don't let a seemingly carefree life keep you from the truth and urgency of this message. And don't let the hopelessness of what you may be going through deceive you into believing that God does not care about you. "Get up;" it is possible! Don't look at your circumstances and see hopelessness, but look to Jesus who calls you to respond to His invitation to healing and freedom. Jesus calls you to "Pick up your mat." Your mat is the evidence of what you are experiencing but is no longer your identity. We often see ourselves as a product of our circumstances, believing we are worthless, disabled, and a failure. It is Satan's powerful weapon to keep us defeated and unable to respond to the truth. "Walk;" bring your pain, sorrow, bitterness, and anger to Jesus so He can take it from you, once for all. Jesus wants you to walk in freedom from the past and from the things that bind you. Often the strongest chains that bind us are mental, emotional, and spiritual, not physical. Are you willing to look beyond your experience and believe what He says? He loves you too much to let you continue on a mat of despair. He calls you to come to Him for the hope you need and the strength to hear His voice in order to obey. Don't hesitate. Do it today!

Chapter Four

When Satan Crushes

When Satan Crushes

Luke 13:10-17 A Crippled Woman is Healed on the Sabbath

"On a Sabbath Jesus was teaching in one of the synagogues, and a woman was there who had been crippled by a spirit for eighteen years. She was bent over and could not straighten up at all. When Jesus saw her, He called her forward and said to her, 'Woman, you are set free from your infirmity.' Then He put His hands on her, and immediately she straightened up and praised God.

Indignant because Jesus had healed on the Sabbath, the synagogue ruler said to the people, 'There are six days for work. So come and be healed on those days, not on the Sabbath.'

The Lord answered him, 'You hypocrites! Doesn't each of you on the Sabbath untie his ox or donkey from the stall and lead it out to give it water? Then should not this woman, a daughter of Abraham, whom Satan has kept bound for eighteen long years, be set free on the Sabbath day from what bound her?'

When He said this, all his opponents were humiliated, but the people were delighted with all the wonderful things He was doing."

Beauty Instead of Ashes

Doctor Luke includes in his gospel of Jesus' life, this intriguing story of Jesus ministering to a woman in an unusual circumstance. In most other settings we see Jesus interact with people who have either sinned or were victims in this fallen world where illness and disease are commonplace. But here we get a glimpse of another cause for suffering – Satan. We don't like talking about Satan but Jesus certainly knew of his existence and it was one reason for His coming: "The reason the Son of God appeared was to destroy the devil's work" (1 John 3:8).

From the scripture we know a few things about this woman. She was a believer, a Jewish woman of faith. On the Sabbath she was in the temple area reserved for Jewish women. We also notice that she was crippled, bent over, and unable to straighten up, and that she had been this way for a long time. Whatever the cause, consider what she might have experienced. Imagine her back bent under a force she could not understand so that little by little her world closed in on her. She probably tried in the beginning, peering up to look people in the eyes even as her head was tilting downward more and more. It required quite an effort to look up which exhausted her energy. Eventually she would be unable to look people straight in the eye and so she must have struggled with hopelessness, discouragement, despair, and a growing sense of fear. She was no doubt conscious of the effect it had on others too; how they would bend down to look her in the face, squatting lower and lower. After a while many would not even try, avoiding her when she came near. She imagined their thoughts, felt their pity, and experienced increasing isolation. The physical pain and growing loneliness was

When Satan Crushes

bad enough, but another pain went deeper still as her spirit began to shrivel. For how many years had she prayed for healing? How many times had she come before the priests to offer sacrifices for sins and offenses that might have caused God to inflict her? When no relief was in sight, did she begin to hear a small voice in her mind whispering ever so subtly, "Why won't God heal? What have I done to deserve this? Is God punishing me?" Every Sabbath she attended the synagogue, dutifully taking her seat with the other women. Quietly she followed tradition, yet her soul ached for relief as her prayers fell silently on the ground. The years went by, hope draining away as her world slowly caved in.

Then one Sabbath Jesus came to the synagogue. He saw her and called her forward. Typically women were not allowed in the central area, much less a crippled woman. But Jesus intentionally called her to come into the restricted space, right up front into that special area reserved only for men. He did it to point out how much He loved her, to show His power to heal, and to the astonishment of many, to defeat the work of the devil. This woman, whom Jesus now spoke to in front of the whole synagogue, might have initially refused and been horrified at what He was commanding. But she obeyed. Hesitantly and slowly she shuffled into the center of everyone's attention. Was she quivering when He spoke, perhaps quaking under the stern judgmental stare of the religious leaders who kept a strict eye on everything within the Jewish community? She heard Jesus' strong yet tender voice say, "Woman, you are set free from your infirmity." Then He placed His hands on her to calm her and to gently lift her face to look into His loving eyes.

Beauty Instead of Ashes

What did she see and feel as she looked up for the first time in eighteen years into the sweet Master's eyes? There is no doubt that she would experience His tender compassion as she saw His encouraging smile and felt His sweet embrace. With new found strength she might have even burst into jubilant praise, similar to that of the Reverend Martin Luther King when he envisioned his day of emancipation; "I'm free, I'm free, praise God Almighty, I'm free at last!"

It is difficult to fathom the synagogue ruler's reaction. With arms folded across his chest he snorted, "There are six days for work. So come and be healed on those days, not on the Sabbath." How dare he interfere with praise to God for a miracle! Imagine how Jesus' face must have changed. From delighting in this woman standing straight and praising God with all her might, He turned to look at the synagogue ruler who scolded her. It is fascinating to hear Jesus' rebuke of the synagogue ruler, for without it we would not have gained this important insight.

The first thing Jesus does is defend her. Stepping between the woman and the synagogue ruler, Jesus looks him straight in the eyes. In a low, controlled voice filled with passion and tinged with righteous anger, He declares the truth, affirming her identity: "She is a daughter of Abraham," and therefore a true believer. Then Jesus clarifies her predicament; her crippling was not what they thought. The Pharisees and religious leaders had a nasty habit of classifying people based on faulty understanding of the Old Testament. They professed that if you suffered illness or calamity it meant you had sinned and deserved judgment. After all, they reasoned, God blessed obedience with rewards and punished disobedience with sorrow and pain. Therefore, this woman must have done something really bad. Furthermore, so as to not interfere with God's judgment, they would keep their distance in order to avoid contaminating themselves with "sinners." It is easy to see how this type of reasoning kept the crippled woman bound in chains of inner pain and torment. In time, she would not question what the religious leaders taught. She would yield to their reasoning. She would feel their added burden of guilt bending her down into despair. No wonder she did not look up, not into the condemnation of the Pharisees, or people's eyes, and especially not into God's eyes.

Ponder for a moment the impact of Jesus' statement regarding this woman's infirmity, that Satan had kept her bound for eighteen long years. Ascribing the source of this woman's pain and misery to Satan was undoubtedly surprising to her and to the religious leaders of her time. Unfortunately, many Christians today are also confused and fail to attribute to Satan much of the evil and suffering that is in the world. They mistakenly reason that in Bible times people were ignorant of science and modern explanations and "saw Satan behind every bush." They naively continue to deny the existence of the supernatural altogether and explain every illness or unexplained phenomena in physical or emotional terms that fit the scientific standard. We will do well to keep in mind that God has graciously allowed scientists to understand and to treat the medical and emotional origins of many disorders such as epilepsy, psychosis and schizophrenia. However, not all seizures, delusions, hallucinations and emotional pain can be explained scientifically. Sometimes there are supernatural causes, which are rooted in Satan's evil nature. An example of God's intervention to overcome Satan's work is found in Luke 8: 26-39 where we read of the sudden change in the man delivered from a legion of demons.

What we need therefore, is a better understanding of the Biblical view of evil and its source, Satan. Not that all bad things are attributed to him, but there is a need to acknowledge that Satan is the author of sin and evil. Conversely, God is the author of all that is good. There are times when we will wrestle with why God allows certain things, or why He does not rid the earth of Satan and evil. Scripture helps us in our search for answers by reminding us of God's gracious love and Satan's evil intent. Otherwise, we would not be able to come alongside people who are suffering and help them deal with their pain and sorrow. When they are at the end of hope, we can remind them of God's unfailing love, no matter what their circumstances. Satan loves to cast the blame on God, that in the painful trial He is uncaring or absent. We would be wise to consider the possibility that Satan is not only behind much of the suffering but that he is the one whispering these destructive lies into their ears. Unless we understand and accept the reality of the spiritual realm we will never fully comprehend the complete picture of some disorders, which include not only a physical and an emotional component but a spiritual one as well. Only then can we offer real hope and healing that is grounded in truth.

When Satan Crushes

A good example of Satan's evil work, which often remains hidden from our understanding, is the story of Job in the Old Testament. With God's permission and with extraordinary malice, Satan was able to touch Job's family, possessions, and even his health. Though much of the agony Job endured was physical, it was difficult emotionally for him to understand why God did not answer his cry for an explanation, for Job was a righteous man. Did Job ever discover that he was the unfortunate victim of Satan's challenge to God? Probably not, which should cause us to also be aware of Satan's subtle yet destructive schemes when we face difficulties.

We cannot blame Satan for everything bad that happens. Just living in this world exposes us to a number of potential catastrophes: germs which cause disease, the natural decay of our bodies, accidents and natural disasters that come our way, and the pain that is so often inflicted by others. Sometimes we experience painful consequences as a result of our own selfish and misguided choices and actions. It is interesting to note that Jesus distinguished between Satan's work and that of illnesses, natural calamities and the consequences of sin. In the case of this crippled woman, Jesus held Satan responsible. But Satan could have used other, indirect methods to cause her crippling. It is helpful therefore, to consider what other ways Satan can inflict suffering that can literally bend people down, robbing them of life and joy.

Satan is well aware that emotions provide quick and easy inroads to our mind, changing the way we think and perceive reality. He knows that if he can control our minds, he can control our lives. Two of the most powerful emotions, shame and guilt, are the byproducts of choices we make to meet our needs in ways that are generally unacceptable or apart from God's will. God designed us to experience these emotions in order to recognize our sin and come to Him for forgiveness and cleansing. Once we acknowledge our sin and confess it to God, He forgives us, wiping away the shame and reversing the separation from Him. These feelings are useful then, in telling us that something is wrong. But Satan also knows that if he can deceive us, he can use shame and guilt to make us feel beyond hope so that we will not come to God in repentance in order to receive God's forgiveness. That kind of separation often continues with tragic results. Read how David describes his struggle with shame and guilt and the effects that sin literally had on his body. In Psalm 38 he writes:

> *"O LORD, do not rebuke me in Your anger, or discipline me in Your wrath.*
> *For Your arrows have pierced me, and Your hand has come down upon me.*
> *Because of Your wrath there is no health in my body; my bones have no soundness because of my sin.*
> *My guilt has overwhelmed me like a burden too heavy to bear. (1-4)*
> *I am bowed down and brought very low; all day long I go about mourning.*
> *My back is filled with searing pain; there is no health in my body.*
> *I am feeble and utterly crushed; I groan in anguish of*

> *heart. (6-8)*
> *My friends and companions avoid me because of my wounds; my neighbors stay far away." (11)*

We do not know the sin that David was struggling with or why he was suffering so intensely. It appeared that instead of quickly recognizing what God desired of him, repentance and confession, David felt overwhelmed because of shame and guilt and therefore felt the heavy hand of God. If David had not eventually recognized God's truth or received godly advice, he could have continued into total despair.

Satan is very aware of the vulnerable condition people are in when they are confronted with their sin and the powerful emotions that result. Unless God's truth is revealed and restoration is accomplished through repentance, a person can experience not only emotional and spiritual crippling, but in time, some sort of physical manifestation as well. The battle takes place in our minds; will we believe what the Bible tells us about God's forgiveness, or will we rely on our feelings and continue to experience the heavy weight of shame and guilt? Satan loves to whisper lies concerning our condition, knowing that if we give in to feelings we can easily be overcome with discouragement and despair. But no matter what we feel, we can experience freedom when we believe what God tells us. When we are restored through God's forgiveness we can enjoy peace and His abundant love. This is the only way to undercut Satan's ability to keep us in bondage, which eventually can cripple us physically, emotionally and spiritually.

Beauty Instead of Ashes

There is another form of crippling, cruel and often silent. Some people have been placed in real prisons due to their sins. Judicial courts have found them guilty and they have served time for their crime. However, some sins society will always find hard to forgive, even though these people have certain rights after serving time or making restitution. The stigmas attached to those released from prison can scar the soul and haunt the mind. These are the burdens they will continue to carry, silent yet heavy enough to crush the spirit. How important it is for us to see these people the way God does: forgiven, cleansed and restored to dignity and value. What they need is to be embraced by God's people, helping them to live in a way that is pleasing to God and to society. But instead, too many former prisoners will struggle alone. Sadly, it will only be a matter of time before many succumb to destructive behavior by seeking relief from the cruel chains that Satan has bound them with.

Tragically, guilt and shame are also closely connected to physical, emotional, or sexual abuse. These types of behaviors often cause confusion as the mind of the victim is tricked into believing that somehow the abuse was deserved. This deception directed by Satan is especially strong and difficult to overcome as it attacks and destroys one's identity. Victims of abuse too easily embrace Satan's lies, believing "I <u>am</u> guilty, I <u>am</u> shameful." Believing such lies slowly and inevitably erodes the ability to enjoy life, resulting in broken and useless lives. In Biblical times and many places today, women continue to endure abuse as they are regarded less important than men and are afforded few rights.

Perhaps the crippled woman in the Bible struggled under this type of abuse, slowly giving in to its weight with no recourse but to buckle under.

Sadly, many children are victims of domestic violence, experiencing the anger and fury unleashed either directly or indirectly by those who should be protecting and providing for them. Homes and schools used to be safe environments for raising children, nurturing healthy and happy families, and providing for stable societies. Today that is the exception and not the norm. How many people today struggle in a similar way, especially if they are poor and have no one to intercede for them? How many carry scars deeper and more painful than physical wounds, scars of the soul that slowly impair the life God intended for them to enjoy. Lingering shame and guilt take its toll, the weight growing heavier even as hope fades, and despair settles in.

Have you had a similar experience? It will only be a matter of time before you hear a small voice inside condemn you. Notice how it affects your posture. Especially if you were brought up in a community of faith you might be troubled by such thoughts as, "Look what you did! How could you do that, being a Christian? What kind of Christian do you think you are, anyway?" Other thoughts might follow, like "What if the pastor knows…maybe he does! Those people talking over there, maybe they know, too. The way they look at me, they must know…" As you listen to these thoughts, you grow quiet, move away and divert your eyes from others. Bowing your head in shame, you avoid certain people, sure they will notice something is not right with you. Even your prayers do not bring you the peace and comfort they used to. Instead you discover Bible verses that speak of condemnation for the sinner. With no relief in sight, you bow your head and bend your back under the burden of shame and guilt.

Could it be that we are too often unaware of Satan's strategy? He comes at just such moments, waiting till we are ripe for his attack of subtle deception, whispering lies in our ear and feeding the fires of our emotions. The tragic effect is separation from God, from the knowledge of His love and forgiveness, and the strength He offers us to persevere and overcome. It is true, of course, that we are responsible for our sin and for confessing it to God, but as children of God, do we realize the burden has been lifted? God loves us, His children, so much that He took the burden of sin, guilt, and shame off each of us and placed it on His Son. It was heavy! It bowed His head and back so much that it broke Him. The amazing truth is that it pleased the Father to do so, so as not to break us. In Isaiah God tells us it was His will to afflict His Son: "Yet it was the Lord's will to crush Him and cause Him to suffer…for He bore the sin of many, and made intercessions for the transgressors" (Isaiah 53:10, 12). Jesus took our guilt and shame and died to forever banish them from us. Satan lies when he tells you your sin is still on your back. These lies can bend you under the weight of shame, down into submission and isolate you from life. Like David, realize your need to call on God, quickly! He is the source of abundant and eternal life through the sacrifice of His Son, who took from you every burden of sin.

When Satan Crushes

Perhaps the woman in the synagogue was crippled due to lies of Satan that bound her under a weight of shame, guilt or despair. When Jesus called her forward in order to free her, He put His hands on her. He did not rebuke her of sin or speak of anything in her past. Jesus' simple yet powerful message to this woman, "You are set free from your infirmity," reminds us that Jesus came to "Proclaim freedom for the captives and prisoners" (Isaiah 61:1, Luke 4:18). Jesus further explained that this woman was a prisoner of Satan, kept in chains that crippled her until her life was one of despair. Satan's strategy is always to destroy, but thank God, Jesus noticed! Once set free from the infirmity caused by Satan, we can only imagine how she felt: the joy of standing tall and walking without pain and the crippling curvature of her back!

Jesus notices you, too. Have you ever felt like this woman? Has guilt or shame robbed you of life, joy, relationships, and freedom? Has it crippled you under a weight and force too great for you to handle? I had a friend who wore a mask of pain. You probably know people like her, pain that is so evident on their face. She tried to hide it but could not. It robbed her of friends, of being carefree in talking, sharing, and relating. She withdrew because of the pain and in her isolation she thought no one would understand and accept her, not even God. Her pain stemmed from guilt but quickly grew through the subtle deception of Satan. It seemed even God kept the spotlight on her past as she kept reading certain Bible verses that condemned her and so the pain increased. Nothing she did seemed to help. She grew desperate. All she wanted was to hear the loving voice of her Father and to experience the peace of forgiveness she knew the Bible spoke of. But instead she heard voices that condemned her, which she erroneously thought was God's voice. That was more than she could bear. She finally ended her life, but really, it was stolen from her. It was Satan's voice she had listened to. She never would have listened had she known it was Satan but she thought it made sense. In her pain, it seemed to be right. Despair. It comes at the end of a long line of words that describe what too many experience: fear, confusion, pain, shame, guilt, and despair. It doesn't happen overnight but slowly, the loss of hope and onset of despair bends the back down, robs the eyes of sight, and steals the joy from life. Heavy doors slam shut on the prisoner who experiences these feelings, but escape and even joy is available through Jesus.

Jesus! Jesus is the name above all names, that at the name of Jesus every knee shall bow but every back will become straight as chains fall off and the prisoner is set free. His Words are life, power, and strength as He says to you, "You are set free of your infirmity." Will you believe Him? Listen to His Words and not the words of the liar, the devil who shackles you with lies. Jesus' Words are true and they will give you life and hope.

I love the reaction of the people. Jesus humiliated His opponents but delighted the people. They witnessed His power over this woman's infirmity. Jesus brought her back into full and abundant life and they shared her joy. Though you were not there this was recorded for you. Jesus knows you, He knows what you are facing right now and He says to you, "Whatever the devil has

When Satan Crushes

told you, do not believe him. No matter what your burden is, it has been lifted off you. I took it to the cross, it has been taken care of forever. You do not need to carry it any longer. I have come to set you free, free to be the child I made you to be. Walk therefore, in freedom and in life."

Chapter Five

The Deepest Healing

The Deepest Healing

Luke 5:17-26   Jesus Heals the Paralytic

"One day as He was teaching, Pharisees and teachers of the law, who had come from every village of Galilee and from Judea and Jerusalem, were sitting there. And the power of the Lord was present for Him to heal the sick. Some men came carrying a paralytic on a mat and tried to take him into the house to lay him before Jesus. When they could not find a way to do this because of the crowd, they went up on the roof and lowered him on his mat through the tiles into the middle of the crowd, right in front of Jesus.

When Jesus saw their faith, He said, 'Friend, your sins are forgiven.'

The Pharisees and the teachers of the law began thinking to themselves, 'Who is this fellow who speaks blasphemy? Who can forgive sins but God alone?'

Jesus knew what they were thinking and asked, 'Why are you thinking these things in your hearts? Which is easier: to say, "Your sins are forgiven," or to say, "Get up and walk?" But that you may know that the Son of Man has authority on earth to forgive sin...' He said to the paralyzed man, 'I tell you, get up, take your mat and go home.'

Immediately he stood up in front of them, took what he had been lying on and went home praising God. Everyone was amazed and gave praise to God. They were filled with awe and said, 'We have seen remarkable things today.'"

Beauty Instead of Ashes

Probably the best-known and loved story of Jesus' healing is this beautiful account of men bringing their paralyzed friend to Jesus. From the beginning of His ministry Jesus attracted large crowds, an interesting mix of believers, scoffers, doubters, and down right antagonists. They came for different reasons. Some came to listen to the Rabbi in love and respect. Some came for healing and comfort. Others came out of curiosity or doubt, and to find out who this Man was. Many came to see a miracle, the best show in town! This occurrence was no different except that it took place in a home, hence the lack of space for everyone to have a good view of Jesus.

At first glance the obvious need of the paralyzed man was for physical healing. But Jesus saw a larger and deeper need. Perhaps on that day He spoke on forgiveness and how important it was for physical, emotional, and spiritual health. If He did, some might have nodded in agreement, remembering how it was true for them. Others might have lowered their heads in shame, remembering the many occasions when they refused to forgive or found it hard to receive forgiveness. The religious leaders probably kept their arms folded across their chests, their stony stares at Jesus never wavering. Jesus knew however, that a powerful display on forgiveness would soon materialize out of thin air, a perfect illustration to His point. Sure enough as He taught, something unusual started happening right over their heads – the roof was caving in! Actually, it was being torn apart until several faces looked right through the opening. The crowd parted just enough to allow the stretcher to reach the floor at Jesus' feet. Interestingly, I

The Deepest Healing

don't think Jesus was surprised but pleased; He had been expecting this man.

Do you think it odd that Jesus' first words to the paralytic were, "Your sins are forgiven?" Undoubtedly it infuriated the religious leaders. You can almost hear them fume under their breath, "Forgiving someone's sins – the impertinence of Him, and a nobody at that! Only God can do this and in our opinion, Jesus is not God." Jesus knew what they were thinking so He startled them with the question, "Why are you thinking these things in your hearts?" As they wondered how He could read their thoughts, He followed with a poignant question, "Which is easier: to say, 'Your sins are forgiven,' or to say, 'Get up and walk'?" Pondering His question they might have surmised that it was easier to say, "Your sins are forgiven," as it is impossible to prove, hence easy to say. To have stopped there though, would have left doubt as to who He was and His authority to forgive. So Jesus healed the man, raising him from his bed of paralysis and proving beyond a shadow of doubt that He was deity. None but deity could forgive and He proved it by healing. The result was a joyous celebration and speechless Pharisees, but was that all? Let's look again at the passage.

When the paralytic was lowered before Jesus, His gaze must have been slow and deliberate. With compassion He assessed the man's condition and found that his needs were profound. Paralysis is one of the dreaded conditions of every age. As a nurse years ago, I worked a few shifts on the spinal cord unit. It was there that the reality of the dreaded diagnosis of spinal cord injury jolts your world with a numbing shock and realization that never again will your loved one walk or use their arms and legs as before. It would haunt my dreams at night, especially when my children first got their driving permits as I imagined them in a car accident with spinal cord injury. I know that life with spinal cord injury does continue and for many it becomes their greatest challenge and accomplishment – to persevere and even to triumph through it. But for a mother or father to view the crippled body of their dear child, would break their hearts and crush their hopes and dreams. Perhaps such was the fate of this man lying paralyzed before Jesus. Jesus could heal this man and restore his shattered dreams. So why did he first say, "Your sins are forgiven?" There are several possibilities.

The medical community acknowledges that perhaps up to 50% of hospital beds today are occupied by those suffering from psychosomatic diseases. These diseases manifest as physical disorders with characteristic symptoms but are actually the result of emotional traumas and stresses. Psychosomatic diseases are not easily diagnosed but it is imperative that a correct diagnosis be made for their recovery. In such cases doctors will diagnose the physical symptoms and prescribe treatment, but surprisingly they will not see the anticipated healing or the alleviation of the symptoms. After several attempts with other remedies and still no improvement, they will consider whether underlying emotional causes might be to blame. What doctors often discover is that if the underlying cause is emotional, then physical healing can occur only when the emotional cause is identified and addressed. This type of intervention often uncovers significant events or traumas from the past, which generate powerful emotional responses. These emotions trigger the development of coping mechanisms, which initially are designed for survival. When dealing with a traumatic event and the resultant emotions such as fear or anger, the mind will often resort to such coping mechanisms as shock, denial, regression, or repression. Almost anything is embraced that appears to lessen or alleviate the emotional pain, which at first can seem overwhelming. But over time, even the coping mechanisms are insufficient to adequately deal with the traumatic event. If left in place, these coping mechanisms themselves can eventually cause degenerative symptoms within the person. Part of the healing process then, is to identify the significant event that triggered the emotional response. The goal is to bring the event into the light, identify the emotional responses and the corresponding coping mechanisms. By gently introducing Biblical truths of Jesus' presence and power to heal, these emotions can be resolved, thereby alleviating the continuing need for the coping mechanisms.

Take for example the alarming rise in violent crime today, which leaves countless victims filled with fear, rage and anger. Many times there is no way to reverse the damage or to gain restitution. The stress of prolonged fear or bitterness can trigger reactions within the body, which may include damaged stomach and intestinal linings, tension headaches and migraines, even arthritis - like symptoms or neurological changes. Could such prolonged stress over time cause a form of crippling and even paralysis? If coping mechanisms are put into place, such as managing the physical or emotional pain through medication, alcohol or drugs, these may offer initial relief. Yet when such powerful emotions are merely covered over, the long term effect can be devastating. The Bible wisely tells us in Ephesians 4:26, "In your anger do not sin. Do not let the sun go down while you are still angry." Verse 32 adds, "Be kind and compassionate to one another, forgiving each other, just as in Christ God forgave you." And in 1 Peter 5: 7 God instructs us to "Cast all your anxiety on Him because He cares for you." God knows when crimes are committed. He sees and He cares enough to instruct the victim to bring to Him all their pain and emotion, allowing His love to gently begin the healing. It is through forgiveness that freedom from the past can happen. Then and only then can healing occur. Holding on to the pain with bitterness and unforgiveness only prolongs the agony and keeps the victim in chains. Perhaps this is why Jesus first dealt with the need for forgiveness with the paralyzed man. Perhaps he had been wounded by someone, grievously hurt and left deeply scarred. In his pain he sheltered it, harbored it and would not let it go. It simmered, then boiled, then controlled his life with unending bitterness. I wonder how many others would be able to rise from a type of paralysis if they would only forgive those who had cruelly hurt them. Forgiveness may not make sense to the victim. Only when they realize what unforgiveness is doing to them, will they find the strength and determination to forgive. For the Christian it begins by coming to the cross where Jesus took all our sins upon Himself, suffered and died as a victim. Once we view the marvelous grace of God to forgive all our sins, then we can find the ability to obey our Lord's command to forgive those who sin against us. Jesus Himself taught His disciples how to pray concerning sin and forgiveness. In Matthew 6: 12 we read, "Forgive us our debts, as we also have forgiven our debtors." By not forgiving others, the disciples would be disobeying their Lord. Do we do likewise? If so, then we need to confess our unwillingness to forgive and allow Jesus to forgive us before then, in obedience, we can forgive others.

Perhaps Jesus saw another reason to forgive this man. Peering into his soul He might have discovered sin that had never been confessed and forgiven. What does unforgiven sin do in a person? It can paralyze and inflict pain to the extent that it literally steals freedom from life. Guilt and shame are powerful, controlling and destructive, driving people to extraordinary measures just to find relief. Self-medicating through overuse of alcohol, pain prescriptions, or illegal drugs in order to lose touch with reality are vain attempts to escape from this type of pain. Adam and Eve experienced guilt and shame for the first time with consequences they never thought possible. The result of sin produced fear of God, so they hid from Him. But God quickly sought them in order to reveal their sin. Had He not, the long term effects of shame and guilt might have driven Adam and Eve even further from the salvation that God freely offered through the sacrifice of an animal. Even David the Psalmist experienced surprisingly powerful symptoms as a result of his sin, which we read about in Psalm 38:

Beauty Instead of Ashes

"For Your arrows have pierced me (2)…
Because of Your wrath there is no health in my body (3)…
My guilt has overwhelmed me like a burden too heavy to bear (4)…
My back is filled with searing pain (7)…
I am feeble and utterly crushed (8)…
My heart pounds, my strength fails me (10)…
For I am about to fall, and my pain is ever with me (17)."

And again, David tells us how the physical symptoms drove him to confession and repentance, in Psalm 32:

"When I kept silent, my bones wasted away through my groaning all day long (3)…
My strength was sapped as in the heat of summer (4).
Then I acknowledged my sin to you and did not cover up my iniquity. I said, 'I will confess my transgressions to the LORD' – and you forgave the guilt of my sin (5)."

We would be correct to assume that David experienced relief after confessing for we know that the Lord forgave him and restored him to fellowship. No wonder Scripture tells us the *Good News*; that the work of Jesus on the cross deals with our sin, guilt, and shame.

"Christ was sacrificed once to take away the sins of many people." Heb 9:28
"Then one of the seraphs flew to me with a live coal in his hand…'See, this has touched your lips; your guilt is taken away and your sin atoned for.'" Isaiah 6:7
"Instead of their shame my people will receive a double portion…for He has clothed me with garments of salvation and arrayed me in a robe of righteousness." Isaiah 61:7, 10

The Deepest Healing

God offers the free gift of eternal life through repentance so you can experience full forgiveness and freedom from guilt, shame, and any other feeling of condemnation that robs you of life and joy. Take His gift of forgiveness. Jesus paid it, once and for all and it is now yours to receive.

There is yet another consideration from this story of Jesus' encounter with the paralyzed man. The Bible assures us of complete forgiveness when we confess our sins to God, for Jesus takes all our sin and guilt to the cross. It is there that God exacts judgment, not on us but on the perfect substitute, Jesus, punishing Him fully for what our sins deserve. But He does not stop there for He extends mercy by clothing us with the righteousness of Jesus, declaring we are forgiven and holy. Even so, many struggle to receive that total forgiveness, the cleansing of their souls, in order to experience peace and acceptance. Many continue to be plagued with guilt and think God cannot or will not forgive them. This deception is from the devil who tells a person lies concerning how God acts and feels toward them. In this confusion there is a tendency to pull away from God and others, hiding because of guilt and shame. Unaware that this is a lie, many continue to withdraw from life and miss out on the freedom that comes from being God's child. Sadly for some, there is no end to the misery and sorrow experienced as a result of this deception.

A few years ago I had a wonderful opportunity to minister in a maximum-security prison through the ministry of Campus Crusade for Christ. Meeting individual women on a weekly basis, I listened to their stories and I began to understand their pain. Many were victims of abuse, neglected and unloved. Reacting to the harshness of life that surrounded them they acted irresponsibly and eventually were arrested for various crimes. None of these women chose the cruel environment they were born into and the consequences they lived with, especially imprisonment. Now locked away, many for long terms and some for life, they felt a paralysis not unlike the man on the stretcher before Jesus. They could do nothing about their present condition. It seemed so cruel and hopeless. Some gave up and retreated into an empty shell. Believing they were helpless, they gave in to despair, becoming nothing more than a lifeless body. Others became hardened and bitter, erecting walls to hide from the realities of life and from their own irresponsibility. But those who were willing to attend Bible study learned of their true identity: they were children of God who were loved and forgiven. And each woman I had the privilege to minister with ultimately said the same thing; "I am so glad God loved me enough to stop me in my tracks and bring me here (prison), for I am freer here than out there (back in their home environment)!" The look on their faces showed that what they discovered was radical and it transformed them, from the inside out.

Freedom through forgiveness! It is what the women in prison learned and experienced with remarkable joy, despite their prison bars. No amount of counseling, behavior modification, positive thinking, or medication can accomplish what God can when He brings to the heart the reality of forgiveness. Shame and guilt connected with sinful actions by others or personal

The Deepest Healing

choices can crush the soul, leaving an empty shell. But the forgiveness accomplished by Jesus on the cross wipes away the weight of sin and brings freedom that is truly revolutionary and life changing. Jesus encountered each of the women in prison, gently bringing them to the foot of the cross where He had died for their sins. This was important for confession of their sinful choices that had robbed them of peace. It was also at the cross that each woman brought all those people who had hurt and abused them, along with all the accumulated years of pain, and laid them all down. It was difficult for some as they would never again see loved ones and never have a chance at freedom. But it was there that Jesus took it all: the sin, guilt, shame, bitterness, despair and depression. Jesus removed it through forgiveness, restored freedom, and gave them back their lives. Jesus released them from their chains of guilt. But sadly, many of these women would carry the label of "convict" all their lives. It is hard to comprehend that God forgives but society often does not. The forgiveness of God is such that He removes our shame and guilt "as far as east is from west, so far has he removed our transgressions from us" Psalm 103:12. In order to drive home this truth, I would tell each woman, "You can go to that guard over there and tell him, 'I don't belong here anymore. I am forgiven, cleansed, declared by God, NOT GUILTY!' That is how God sees you, forgiven and your punishment paid in full!" The smile on her face and the twinkle in her eye would tell me that she understood! That's true freedom!

Unfortunately, we cannot see the look on the paralytic's face when Jesus spoke of forgiveness. If he was burdened by the weight and guilt of unforgiven sin,

Beauty Instead of Ashes

then the look on his face would have registered relief and joy. If he had struggled with believing and receiving forgiveness, hearing it from Jesus would have broken any doubt and shattered any stronghold. If he was unaware of sin and guilt, he might have looked surprised or confused: "What are you talking about, forgiving my sin? What does that have to do with me or what I am suffering with?" The paralytic might have thought he was correct, yet the deepest need of everyone is forgiveness, whether they know it or not. Whatever the man's state of mind and soul, once Jesus said, "Your sins are forgiven" he was able to receive physical healing; he was free to get up and walk. Truly, what was even more remarkable, he was now fully forgiven! When Jesus forgives, no matter what the sin, guilt or shame, God says "Their sins ... I will remember no more" Hebrews 10:17. Not that God literally forgets for He is omniscient, knowing all things. What it means is He will never hold the guilt to our account; He will never remember it to use it against us. That is true forgiveness that brings healing and freedom! Jesus' mandate at the beginning of His public ministry recorded in Luke 4:17-19, is taken from Isaiah 61: 1-3, 4. Its words are true for us today:

> *"The Spirit of the Lord is on me, because He has anointed Me to preach good news to the poor.*
> *He has sent Me to proclaim freedom for the prisoners and recovery of sight for the blind,*
> *To release the oppressed, to proclaim the year of the Lord's favor.*
> *They will rebuild the ancient ruins and restore the places long devastated;*

The Deepest Healing

They will renew the ruined cities that have been devastated for generations."

What a wonderful passage showing Jesus' purpose to rebuild, restore, and renew lives that were devastated, destroyed, torn down or apart by sin's awful consequences. This man was healed and restored; he was made as new once his sins were forgiven!

Healing comes in many forms but always in order. This story of healing from the Gospels was both spiritual and physical. Jesus did not mix the order. First came the spiritual healing from sin's effect, which not only cripples but also kills the soul. Once forgiveness restores the soul, physical healing can begin just as Jesus spoke those incredible words "I tell you, get up, take your mat and go home." Keep in mind, not every illness is due to sin and physical healing may not always follow forgiveness. But it might. Would you search your soul right now to consider what God might be showing you? David the Psalmist shows us how, in Psalm 139:23-24: "Search me, O God, and know my heart; test me and know my anxious thoughts. See if there is any offensive way in me, and lead me in the way everlasting."

Chapter Six

The Crushing Blow

of Accusation

The Crushing Blow of Accusation

John 8:2-11 Jesus Forgives An Adulteress

"At dawn He appeared again in the temple courts, where all the people gathered around Him, and He sat down to teach them. The teachers of the law and the Pharisees brought in a woman caught in adultery. They made her stand before the group and said to Jesus, 'Teacher, this woman was caught in the act of adultery. In the Law Moses commanded us to stone such women. Now what do you say?' They were using this question as a trap, in order to have a basis for accusing Him.

But Jesus bent down and started to write on the ground with His finger. When they kept on questioning Him, He straightened up and said to them, 'If any one of you is without sin, let him be the first to throw a stone at her.' Again He stooped down and wrote on the ground.

At this, those who heard began to go away one at a time, the older ones first, until only Jesus was left, with the woman still standing there. Jesus straightened up and asked her, 'Woman, where are they? Has no one condemned you?'

'No one, sir,' she said.

'Then neither do I condemn you,' Jesus declared. Go now and leave your life of sin.'"

Beauty Instead of Ashes

Many have been blessed through this story, a beautiful demonstration of the mercy and the grace that Jesus showed to this woman. For though there was a basis for judgment, Jesus instead showed mercy by not giving her what she deserved, which was punishment, and grace by giving her what she did not deserve, which was forgiveness. After all, to forgive was His prerogative as long as He did not overlook the demands for justice and righteousness. He viewed this woman as God the Father did, with love for her even in her sin and a willingness to save her, both physically and spiritually. With the distant view of the cross in mind Jesus forgave her, knowing that He Himself would take her sin and guilt and on the cross He would fully satisfy the demands of a holy and a righteous God.

The scene before us is also a graphic portrayal of the religious leaders in their harsh judgment and their devious schemes. A frightened woman is thrown to the ground at the feet of Jesus, apparently having just been dragged from a bed of passion and adultery. Her long hair is now loose around her bare shoulders as she clutches the bed sheet that was hastily drawn about her naked body. Helpless and ashamed she is surrounded by the teachers of the law and Pharisees in their ornate robes and long prayer shawls. These were holy men on a mission of justice, pointing fingers of accusation down upon her shaking body. She was guilty. Even Moses would have charged her and fulfilled the law that demanded punishment. But something was not right. It was obviously a set-up. The teachers of the law and the Pharisees were trying to trap Jesus by accusing Him of being unfair in His judgment of the woman. In reality,

The Crushing Blow of Accusation

they were the ones who were unfair by bringing just the woman before their little tribunal. Didn't it say she was "caught in the act of adultery?" Then where was the man and why was he not also put on trial? If Jesus had agreed with them and joined in casting stones, they would have turned the tables and accused Him of being unfair.

Rather than fall for their trap and argue with them or try to point out the hypocrisy of their scheme, Jesus started writing on the ground. Some speculate He was writing some of the commandments listed in Exodus 20:1-17. The teachers and Pharisees would have expected Him to write the seventh one, "You shall not commit adultery." More than likely, Jesus might have written the sixth commandment, "You shall not murder" or even the ninth, "You shall not give false testimony against your neighbor." Yes, they had cause to judge her but not by their standards, which were not in her best interest. God's judgments were never given to condemn but to reveal truth and to bring all to repentance leading to salvation as seen in John 3:17, "For God did not send His Son into the world to condemn the world but that the world through Him might be saved." In 2 Peter 3: 9 it also says about God, "He is patient with you, not wanting anyone to perish, but everyone to come to repentance." If Jesus had written either the sixth or ninth commandments that might reveal why the men who were seeking His approval to stone her slowly dispersed, the older and wiser ones first.

As those who had accused her left, one by one, the woman stood alone before Jesus. Jesus did not disagree with the charge they had brought against her. He saw she was frightened and helpless. Those who accused her had wanted to destroy her. He loved her and desired to save her. There is a wonderful parallel in the Old Testament, which perhaps Jesus also might have written on the ground. It is from Zechariah 3:1-5:

> *"Then he showed me Joshua the high priest standing before the angel of the Lord, and Satan standing at his right side to accuse him. The Lord said to Satan, 'The Lord rebuke you, Satan! The Lord, who has chosen Jerusalem, rebuke you! Is not this man a burning stick snatched from the fire?'*
>
> *Now Joshua was dressed in filthy clothes as he stood before the angel. The angel said to those who were standing before him, 'Take off his filthy clothes.'*
>
> *Then He said to Joshua, 'See, I have taken away your sin, and I will put rich garments on you.'*
>
> *Then I said, 'Put a clean turban on his head.' So they put a clean turban on his head and clothed him, while the angel of the Lord stood by."*

This vision was given to Zechariah the prophet when the exiles returned to Jerusalem from captivity in Babylon. Joshua was the High Priest at the time, the representative of the people before God. As was the custom, he would have been dressed in the cleanest of robes as he presented offerings before a holy God, fearful that any impurity would receive swift judgment from God. The vision gives a clearer picture of what really happened each time the High Priest stood before God. As he approached the Holy of Holies, a courtroom scene of epic proportions was being played out. Consider the

The Crushing Blow of Accusation

players: the Lord presides as Judge to Whom all heaven and earth are accountable. Joshua the accused, represents all people, guilty because of sin and standing before a holy God. Satan the accuser, stands before God but points toward Joshua with vengeance, for he is loaded with evidence. But notice another is present, referred to as "The angel of the Lord." Many commentators think this is Jesus, an Old Testament manifestation of God revealed in His unique role as Savior and Defender. It is before this angel of the Lord that Joshua stands. It is amazing to see the audacity of Satan, to stand before God and point his finger of accusation toward God's High Priest. But he had every right to do so. Joshua was guilty. As the representative of us all, he truly was dressed in filthy rags. What right do any of us have to stand before a holy God and think we can escape His righteous judgment and our deserved punishment? But instead of the righteous Judge handing down condemnation, He rebukes the accuser! God would never give a judgment that was not perfect, so we are shown why He will not condemn and destroy Joshua. The angel, probably Jesus, gives the command to have Joshua's filthy clothes removed, telling Joshua that He has removed his sin. Then Joshua is clothed with rich garments and a clean turban is placed on his head, also pictured in Isaiah 61; 10;

> *"I delight greatly in the LORD; my soul rejoices in my God. For He has clothed me with garments of salvation and arrayed me in a robe of righteousness, as a bridegroom adorns his head like a priest, and as a bride adorns herself with her jewels."*

Beauty Instead of Ashes

God commanding, Jesus providing, and Joshua receiving that which enabled him to stand up to all the accusations of Satan. What a beautiful picture of all that God desires to do for us. It is the Almighty's desire to remove the guilt of our sin while clothing us with His righteous robes, all on the basis of Jesus' death and resurrection. But also notice the disappearance of Satan once the filthy garments are removed and the clean ones are applied. Once the basis for guilt and accusation was removed, Satan had no grounds to continue his accusation. He had been rebuked by the Lord Himself and put in his place.

Consider how this mirrored what the adulterous woman was experiencing. She was guilty, accused, and awaiting punishment. The accusers, the teachers of the law are circling her, heaping charges and guilt upon her. The woman stands in filthy clothes and is speechless. But God commands Jesus, His Representative, to reveal the heart of God and to provide what she needs. First Jesus defends her by challenging the accusers to judge her only if they themselves were without sin. This levels the ground as none are found sinless and the accusers slip away, one by one. Now Jesus and the woman are alone. It says He stooped down and wrote again. Perhaps this time it was for her eyes only. Maybe He wrote the verse from Isaiah 53:12 about the Messiah who would take on the sins of the world; "For He bore the sin of many, and made intercession for the transgressors," or perhaps the verse of how He would clothe His people as a bride with robes of righteousness and jewels (Isaiah 61:10). Whatever He wrote, it accomplished what He wanted. First her filthy clothes were removed when she put her

The Crushing Blow of Accusation

faith in this Man who showed her the truth. He then clothed her Himself, as one receiving the righteous standing of being forgiven and cleansed. In that brief interchange Jesus ministered to her soul. He brought her forgiveness and cleansing, He provided a covering of righteousness and He set her free. She was required to do nothing except leave her life of sin. All else was provided. How she must have marveled at the power of His gaze, not of condemnation but of pure love!

A number of years ago, our daughter Jen was getting married. She was our first to marry so she and I were eager to experience all the joys of planning a wedding. One of the first things we tackled was looking for the perfect dress, the most important part of every bride's dreams. We had heard stories of searching through endless stores so we expected this to be fun but also demanding. A friend gave us an advertisement from an exclusive store that was selling many of their bridal gowns for up to 80% off! It seemed too good to be true but we thought, "Why not try?" It was the first of what we thought would be many outings.

That afternoon we entered the store and were greeted by exquisitely appointed women, eager to demonstrate why they were superior to all other bridal stores in town. Jen was entranced by the number of beautiful gowns all begging to be tried on. She started gathering them up in her arms, intending not to miss one. At that moment a lovely young woman approached Jen and offered to hold each dress she had selected. The woman gathered the growing number of gowns in her arms and led Jen to the dressing room, which was beyond our wildest imagination. It was a huge room encircled by walls of mirrors and in the center of the room was a pedestal. The woman hung the gowns on a rack while I backed into a corner, determined not to say a word but only to watch. Jen was dressed in blue jeans and a faded sweatshirt; her hair was pulled up in a carefree bun. The woman offered to help Jen try on each gown. Jen took off her old, faded clothes as the woman selected a gown and gathered it up in her arms. Jen, being shy and modest, seemed uncomfortable on the pedestal as the woman approached her with the first gown. From the corner I watched in amazement as my daughter was transformed. Jen went from ordinary to regal as the woman expertly guided the gown over Jen's head and swiftly gathered it from behind. Jen literally glowed as she saw herself in the full-length mirrors that reflected her beauty all around. Her hair, still piled on top of her head, no longer looked careless but elegant as her face took on royalty. She reveled in what she saw and I cried! It is truly a miracle how a bride turns into a princess, for the gown tells them what they have always wanted to hear, '"You are beautiful, you are worthy of love!" It is the same for me for Jesus tells me everyday in my walk with Him, "You are beautiful, you are loved, you are clothed in My royal robes of righteousness. I made you what you are, a child of the King!"

 This woman caught in adultery felt nothing but shame and guilt. She did not fight the accusations or the judgment. She prepared herself for death for she deserved it. But Jesus saw her differently. He saw her sin but offered her pardon. He recognized her guilt but offered her cleansing. He took the filthy clothes off her

The Crushing Blow of Accusation

and dressed her in His own righteousness, which He would soon secure by His death on the cross. He set her free. Jesus desires to do the same for you. Will you look into His eyes to see the love that is there? Allow Him to free you from your shame and guilt and to clothe you with His royal robes of righteousness. He is waiting for you; His arms are open wide.

Part 2

When Life

Does Not Make Sense

Chapter Seven

When God Deliberately

Sends Trials:

*A Thorn,
A Stone,
A Dungeon*

Beauty Instead of Ashes

It is a wonderful thing to live for God, devoting your whole life in gratitude and service for His great gift of salvation. Being in full time ministry, my husband and I have personally experienced this blessing and have known many who also have heard the call of God and responded. It is wonderful to walk by faith trusting that as we obey and minister to others, God will supply our own needs. Scripture seems to confirm that those who trust Him will lack nothing as the Psalmist proclaims, "The Lord is my Shepherd, I shall lack nothing" Psalm 23:1. Elsewhere we read that God surrounds His people with a hedge of protection (Job 1:10) and that He blesses those who walk not in the ways of the world but who delight in His law (Psalm 1:1-2). So can you explain why - when you are living for God and depending on His care and provision - life suddenly comes crashing down? For some people this sudden "pulling of the rug out from under their feet" catches them off guard and their faith takes a tumble. Desperately they ask, "Did God withdraw His protection or His blessing from me? Was He unable to control the circumstances?" Even harder to answer are questions like these: "Did God watch from the sidelines when someone abused me? Where was He? Does He care?" It is especially hard to accept that perhaps God deliberately sends physical, emotional or spiritual trials. Did you deserve them? How do you handle these trials? Job wrestled with similar questions for he had no way of knowing that God withdrew His "hedge of protection" (Job 1:10) and allowed Satan to

When God Deliberately Sends Trials

give him a taste of his destructive power. Job adamantly refused to admit sin as the basis for what seemed to be God's punishment. It was what his friends counseled him to do. Try as he might, Job could find no reason for the pain he suffered. For the next 37 chapters Job's cry was for justice; demanding and pleading with God to justify His seemingly unfair treatment of His faithful servant. Even at the end of the book it is doubtful Job's questions were fully answered, yet he appeared to be content with what God did reveal. Are we to expect any more? Let's see what some Bible personalities can show us. We are going to be looking at three people from the Bible whose stories shed important insight into the disappointments of life. These three people are the apostle Paul from the New Testament and from the Old Testament, Isaac's son Jacob and his son Joseph. We will first look at their dilemmas, the trials of life that came upon them seemingly out of nowhere. Then we will follow their search for answers and hopefully we will learn some important lessons for our own lives. So, what are we to learn when the thorn digs, the stone is unyielding, and our righteous actions are rewarded with pain? First, Paul's story.

Paul's dilemma; When the thorn digs.

Paul's life is intriguing. We learn from the book of Acts and from Paul's own letters of his previous way of life as a Pharisee. He was wholly devoted to Judaism and to God. But all that changed when on his way to Damascus he abruptly encountered Jesus. As a result, his eyes were opened to the true nature of his devotion, which was actually opposed to God's will. The one who had once maliciously and zealously opposed Christianity now vehemently championed Jesus as the true Messiah from God. He dearly paid for it too, with life-long persecution from the hands of those he had once been in league with, and with eventual martyrdom.

There was yet another battle Paul faced in addition to the ongoing persecution for Jesus' sake. In 2 Corinthians 12:7 Paul reveals an inner struggle he was wrestling with, finally recognizing its source; a "thorn in the flesh, a messenger of Satan, to torment me." Paul was an accomplished apostle of Jesus, zealously doing the work and will of God. But he was also tormented with something that apparently interfered enough with his life that he begged three times for God to remove it. A "thorn in the flesh" does not seem so great a trial when compared to some of the persecutions Christians have had to endure. It is also amazing how Paul made very little of the severe trials he had endured, briefly mentioning them in 2 Corinthians 11:23-27:

> *"…been in prison more frequently, been flogged more severely, exposed to death again and again, five times received the forty lashes minus one, three times beaten with rods, once stoned, three times shipwrecked, a night and day in open sea, in danger from rivers, bandits…gone without sleep, known hunger and thirst, cold and naked."*

When God Deliberately Sends Trials

Who of us could have handled mistreatment like that without fervent cries and petitions for God to take it away, or at least to do away with those who were mistreating us? But not Paul! Not once do we see him in prayer asking for deliverance, much less for vindication. Perhaps he remembered when he had been a major part of the oppression of Christians, for now he understood the reality of persecution. If Paul could endure such cruel treatment, then why did he voice his complaint in prayer for God to remove this "thorn in his flesh?" Though none of the above trials affected his zeal for God, this thorn had apparently brought him to his knees.

Jacob's dilemma; The unyielding stone.

We read of Jacob's story in the Old Testament in Genesis 27-28. But first as background to Jacob's life, Genesis 12:1-3 recounts his grandfather Abram's long journey from his country to go to a new country, in obedience to God's command but also with God's promises. These promises were to provide a land in which God would build a new nation, and descendents who would be as numberless as the stars in the sky and the sands on the seashore. While in this new country, Abram had two sons; the younger son, Isaac, was chosen by God to inherit the promises that had first been given to Abram (Genesis 21). To Isaac and his wife Rebecca were born twin sons, but again, it was the second-born, Jacob, who was chosen by God to inherit the promises. Even before his birth his mother had been told in a dream that the "older will serve the younger" (Genesis

25:23). Jacob inherited the covenant promises of God and the security provided by God's protection (Genesis 12:2-3). It seemed Jacob had it all handed to him on a "silver platter." So the last thing we expect to see is Jacob fleeing from his brother Esau who threatened to kill him! Not trusting the Word of the Lord given to his mother, Jacob had resorted to his own devises. First he stole the birthright of Esau. Then he deceived his brother and his father, and was now running for his life. But wasn't he the one chosen, even before birth, to be God's vessel through whom the promises to Abraham and Isaac would be fulfilled? Then why was this chosen son of the promise now running alone in the wilderness, without protection, provision, or a clue of what was next? No man of such position and standing in his culture would be without bodyguard, ample provisions, and careful planning for where he was going. But here he was, in a god-forsaken desert with nothing to even sleep on except a stone. How could this be part of God's plan?

Joseph's dilemma; Righteousness rewarded with pain.

We now look at Joseph, perhaps the best example of someone who did not deserve the mistreatment he received. Genesis 29-30 tells the ongoing story of Jacob, how he fathered twelve sons through his two wives and two concubines. Sadly it tells of his dysfunctional parenting style, but also the miraculous way God brought the nation of Israel into existence through these twelve sons. It was God's intent to bless the whole world through the family line of Jacob, for from Israel would be

When God Deliberately Sends Trials

born the Messiah, Jesus. Joseph's story stands out as it shows that God's sovereign plan and purpose can not be thwarted, no matter what circumstances seem to threaten or to interfere.

Joseph was the eleventh-born son of Jacob but the first born of his beloved wife, Rachel. Joseph was spoiled so might have deserved the teasing and ridicule from the older and often overlooked brothers. But to be sold into slavery, a known death sentence, was certainly not deserved. Only by seeing from the vantage point of history can we fully comprehend and appreciate the sovereign hand of God, orchestrating events according to His will. God was with Joseph even as he was taken into Egypt to serve Potiphar's family, but how could Joseph have known this? Over many years of hard service Joseph stayed faithful to His God, though he endured repeated abuse, false accusations by Potiphar's wife for sexual harassment, and years of unfair imprisonment. As Joseph languished in prison he hung on to the slim hope of acquittal from a grateful, yet forgetful fellow servant, the cupbearer (Genesis 40:23). Countless prayers, frustrations, discouragement and silence from heaven must have sorely tested his faith. Who could have endured as much and been as uncomplaining and faithful as Joseph was?

Three men, three stories, and three examples of how life can be so unfair. How many can also say that you have experienced a thorn in the flesh: perhaps a physical ailment, or a diagnosis that threatens to overwhelm you, or a crushing blow that knocks the wind out of you? You cry out to God, not three times but three hundred times, but still no answer. You plead, beg, threaten, bargain, sob and still – nothing. Paul was there. Or have you found yourself lost or confused, running from an enemy, plagued with fear, and threatened by tragedy? Have you lost everything like many hurricane, war, or poverty victims, having only the clothes on your back? Jacob can relate to that sinking feeling of despair. Or have you ever been falsely accused and convicted, the best years of the prime of your life wasted because of another's' jealousy or cruel wrath? Joseph would have a lot to say to you! What can we learn from these men, real people who wrestled with God?

Paul's breakthrough.

Though Paul did not pray for deliverance from those who were harshly persecuting him, he did pray to God for deliverance from the "thorn," whatever it was. And apparently Paul did get an answer from God, only he must not have liked it. So he kept asking, perhaps rephrasing it to clarify just what he was going through. You know the drill, "God, maybe You were napping when I cried out to You. Maybe You do not understand what I am going through, so let me say it again, GET ME OUT OF THIS!" God's reply was the same three times: "My grace is sufficient for you, for My power is made perfect in weakness" (2 Corinthians 12:9). You see, with God there are no mistakes. He made Paul and gave him an area of weakness in his life, even allowing Satan to inflict him there. When that interfered with his life, it became a stumbling block. That stumbling block momentarily rocked Paul's world. From Paul's viewpoint it was not a good thing, so he asked God to get rid of it. Could God have? Absolutely! But He chose not to, allowing it to test Paul. Apparently, Satan took notice too.

In the midst of trials we are vulnerable to the subtle lies of the devil who takes the trial and twists it, perhaps to make us believe that God is against us, absent, or unconcerned. It can be devastating when we are faced with these growing doubts. We struggle with thoughts and beliefs that seem to contradict what we know to be true of God: His love, His compassion, and His power to defend and deliver us from all evil. It is interesting to note that Paul could accept fierce persecutions from men, near-death experiences, and the loss of everything that had been near and dear to him. Then what was it that tormented him so, this "thorn in the flesh"? We may never fully know but from how Paul described it, let's consider what it might have been. What would have been unbearable to Paul? Certainly not persecution, for he had endured everything that had been thrown at him. Perhaps then it was something from within, something that interfered with his ability to hear God's voice, to know of His love and guidance, and to experience His comforting presence. If Satan had been able to interject into Paul's mind a doubt, a lie or a deception so that he began to believe it, would that not have reduced this giant to helplessness? To wrestle with the apparent absence of God's love or approval would certainly have brought Paul torment. Perhaps in his frequent journeys, sometimes barely able to escape a mob of angry people, or especially during the times he was in prison, did he battle the inner doubts that assailed him, nagging, jabbing and tearing at his faith? Did Paul ever whisper in confusion, "Is this really Your will for me, Lord? Am I crazy to keep believing, seeing what I go through? Are You really there, Jesus?" How dark the night is when your prayers are answered with silence and heaven's doors seem locked and barred.

Martin Luther suffered from a similar plight. He struggled for years with guilt and a nagging sense of falling short of God's demands for righteousness. Those haunting, inner doubts that assailed his soul were more fearsome than the growing number of people who sought to take his life because of his criticism of the established church. Luther's journals were filled with agonizing prayers that were often met with silence. That silence reduced him to deep bouts of depression in which he recalled hearing the sneer of the devil. In the painful trial of doubt, when few understand the darkness of despair, the sinister whispers of Satan can be heard, loud and clear. Like Luther, such might have been Paul's inner turmoil: his fierce battle against the arrows of Satan's lies and his growing sense of futility. Only when God revealed to Paul the reason for the thorn – humility and dependence – was he finally able to embrace it. Though

When God Deliberately Sends Trials

Paul was still prone to Satan's lies that could lead to discouragement, God used this weakness to remind him to never depend on or to trust in his own abilities, even as accomplished as he was. Rather than give in to defeat and despair, Paul fully depended on God to accomplish all He intended, which Paul voiced in Philippians 1:20-21: "I eagerly expect and hope that I will in no way be ashamed, but will have sufficient courage so that now as always Christ will be exalted in my body, whether by life or by death. For to me, to live is Christ and to die is gain." With such confidence, no "thorn," even from Satan, could defeat Paul. Because Paul stopped praying for God to remove the thorn, we can surmise that this "thorn" remained in his body, a messenger from Satan that continued to remind Paul to stay humble and dependent on God.

Paul further instructs us in Romans 12: 2, what the key to victory is: "Be transformed by the renewing of your mind." When we are overwhelmed with looming peril or disaster our mind struggles to comprehend and we plead, "Why, Lord?" Being vulnerable, we can be bombarded with lies from the enemy that confuse our ability to see the truth. The only way to gain the higher ground is for truth to be remembered and embraced. David exemplified this well, in 2 Samuel 22: 2-7. When Saul was threatening his life, David remembered this of the Lord:

> *"The Lord is my rock, my fortress and my deliverer;*
> *my God is my rock, in whom I take refuge,*

and my savior – from violent men You save me.
I call to the Lord, who is worthy of praise,
and I am saved from my enemies.
The waves of death swirled about me;
The torrents of destruction overwhelmed me.
The cords of the grave coiled around me;
The snares of death confronted me.
In my distress I called to the Lord; I called out to my God.
From his temple He heard my voice; my cry came to His ears."

David again reminds us of the truth to be remembered in the days of testing, in Psalm 46: 1-3:

"God is our refuge and strength, an ever present help in trouble.
Therefore we will not fear,
Though the earth give way and the mountains fall into the heart of the sea,
Though its waters roar and foam and the mountains quake with their surging."

Little do we like to consider that we also might carry "thorns", painful reminders that test us and reveal our deepest fear, "Is God really trustworthy?" In the midst of our darkest fear, wrestling with the possibility of abandonment, will we trust Him? Would we be as open to receive an answer to prayer as Paul was and be content with it? How do we fight these doubts when they are often immaterial and make no sense yet affect us so profoundly? Does the grace of God sometimes keep us in

When God Deliberately Sends Trials

a painful place where we are constantly reminded, as a thorn would get our attention, that God is faithful and our role is to be humble and dependant? Though we don't relish it, it is something we should recognize and learn to accept from His hands. And remember, if God allows Satan to bring anything into our lives, it is to test us, to refine us, to conform us to His image, and to remind us of His protection and provision as we depend on Him. With that insight we can trust God and praise Him. Remember, Paul continued to learn this lesson. Resolutely, he would lean on God, right up until the day of his martyrdom.

Jacob's perspective.

Jacob was fleeing for his very life, running through the desert in the middle of the night. Genesis 27:41-43 tells us why:

"Esau held a grudge against Jacob because of the blessing his father had given him. He said to himself, 'The days of mourning for my father are near; then I will kill my brother Jacob.' When Rebekah was told what her older son Esau had said, she sent for her younger son Jacob and said to him, 'Your brother Esau is consoling himself with the thought of killing you. Now then, my son, do what I say: Flee at once...'"

Can you imagine your mother telling you, with fear in her eyes, "Run as fast as you can! Flee before it is too late!" Emotional fear is much more exhausting than physical exertion. Only when Jacob was far enough into the emptiness of the desert, well out of harm's way, did he slow down. Weariness had finally caught up with him, so he found a spot to lie down for the night. He must have been very tired for he laid his head on a stone! Jacob had run so fast that in his haste he had not packed a travel bag with provisions. Instead he had to settle for what he found. That hard, cold stone represented all the plans that had gone wrong. In spite of being the favored and beloved son of Isaac and Rebecca and the one through whom the covenant promises of God would be fulfilled, now all he had to his name was a stone, and a hard one at that! But sleep he did, and God entered his dream.

I want you to picture God watching Jacob, patiently waiting for him to finally stop running long enough to get his attention. At the end of a long and weary day, with his head on a stone for a pillow, God spoke to him in a dream: "I will do for you all that I promised your forefather, and count on it, I will bring you back to the land you are running from" (Genesis 28:15). God's promise encompassed all of Jacob's fears, for his present situation did not hold much hope for a bright future. What was Jacob's response? "If you will… then you will be my God" (Genesis 28:20-21). How small was his faith in God, but how patient God was with him. This is very important to grasp: for Jacob to see this trial as God intended, he had to see it from God's perspective. The dream got Jacob's attention, but what he did the next morning showed that he was now seeing it from a

When God Deliberately Sends Trials

different viewpoint. "Early the next morning, Jacob took the stone he had placed under his head and set it up as a pillar and poured oil on top of it. He called that place Bethel" (Genesis 28:18). It had been a hard and cruel pillow the night before, but now it was an altar where God met with him and spoke to him. The stone, illustrating his harsh circumstances, did not change. But when Jacob viewed the stone from God's point of view, when he turned it from laying flat to now standing upright, it became an altar. No longer just a stone, it was "Bethel", or house of God. Jacob was seeing the stone from a different viewpoint, from God's perspective, which helped him also to see his present circumstances from God's perspective. The text does not indicate but I think the ladder from heaven that appeared in his dream and on which he saw angels ascending and descending, touched the very stone he had slept on. Jacob was right when he said that the place where he was sleeping was "the house of God, the gate of heaven." No wonder he took that stone, set it up and poured oil on it. It was his token of worship.

When we encounter difficult circumstances we often perceive them as evil, certainly not part of God's will and a threat to our goals. So we petition God to remove them, thinking God would also agree with our keen insight and wise request. But scripture exhorts us in 1 Peter 5:6, to "Humble yourselves, therefore, under God's mighty hand." When God exerts pressure it is to refine us, not to destroy us. It is hard to find yourself in a desert, where all you had is taken from you and what you have left is a stone. It is hard to come to an end of yourself, where you are finally willing to see God's point of view. Few come willingly. But do we miss the awesome experience of worship, taking the bitter gall of our broken lives and lifting it up for God to receive and redeem? Until we are willing we will never see it from God's perspective, to see what He is doing in it. It takes faith to see God in it, to trust Him to take our precious life and refine it through the fiery trial. But when we do, allowing God to do His work and finish the refining, we will experience the rest of what Peter was speaking of, "that He may lift you up in due time," for all to see (1Peter 5:6). His perfect plan in our lives is to shape us into the person He intended us to be. Can we stop long enough to see His perspective, to turn the stone of despair and see it as a platform for worship?

Joseph's perfecting.

Joseph was wrenched from the safety and security of his home when he was probably in his early teens. He spent the best years of his life as a slave, servant and convict before he was elevated to the status of second in command of the mighty empire, Egypt. No doubt the temptation of anger, hatred and bitterness filled his lonely hours, days, weeks, months and years as he languished alone and forgotten. Yet he chose to rely on His God, confident that He had not forgotten him.

When God Deliberately Sends Trials

Joseph's story illustrates that perhaps the hardest trial anyone faces is to choose to forgive. Unforgiveness is the cancer that slowly but progressively destroys from the inside out. To forgive means to let go of any and every reason to hate, seek revenge and act out of your pain. Who did Joseph need to forgive? There were so many: his father, brothers, Potiphar and his wife, the cupbearer, even God! But Joseph forgave them all and God rewarded him. God could use such a person to bring about great blessing. Though scripture does not tell us of Joseph's actual forgiveness, I believe his demeanor with his brothers reveals he had forgiven those who had hurt him the most. When he could have acted with vengeance and meted out punishment on his brothers, he chose to forgive, recognizing God's purpose through it all; "You intended to harm me, but God intended it for good to accomplish what is now being done, the saving of many lives" (Genesis 50:20). How was Joseph able to persevere through all he endured and come out "smelling like a rose?" Perhaps he remembered the lessons his father Jacob had learned and had taught to his favorite son: lessons learned over the years, that God was a trustworthy God who watched over His people to bring about His promises, no matter what. Perhaps Joseph determined not to be stubborn or foolhardy and seek his own will as his father had, but to submit and to trust God, even when it seemed impossible.

Such persistent faith is surely tested and rewarded, but it still comes at a cost. The question is, is it worth it? I

Beauty Instead of Ashes

believe God encouraged Joseph in his lonely prison as he had no one else. He remembered his earlier dreams that somehow God was going to use him in such a way as to bring him honor. When God looks for one to use in a powerful way, God will test them to produce the character needed. There is a poem pertaining to spiritual leadership learned through suffering that mirrors what Joseph endured:

"When God wants to drill a man
And thrill a man
And skill a man,
When God wants to mold a man
To plan the noblest part;
When He yearns with all His heart
To create so great and bold a man
That all the world shall be amazed,
Watch His methods, watch His ways!

How He ruthlessly perfects
How He royally elects!
How He hammers him and hurts him,
And with mighty blows converts him
Into trial shapes of clay which
Only God understands;
While his tortured heart is crying
And he lifts beseeching hands!

When God Deliberately Sends Trials

*How he bends but never breaks
When his good He undertakes;
How He uses whom He chooses
And with every purpose fuses him;
By every act induces him
To try His splendor out –
God knows what He's about!"*

Author Unknown

Does God likewise deal with us through trials? Does God allow Satan to inflict pain and disability? Does He put hard stones under us or in our way? Does God torment us with fear or loneliness or despair? I believe He does. Are we aware of what God is doing? Most times we are not. But we can expect that God will speak to us in the pain, especially when we take the time to look at it from God's perspective, to see what He is doing in and through it.

The conclusion

Paul was not only able to endure incredible persecution but also to glory in his weakness. He had learned through good times and bad, that God was His strength and defender. Paul knew what it was like to be oppressed by the enemy and in those times to lean totally on God. Humbly, Paul submitted to whatever God brought into his life, for he knew that God would be glorified in it, even in his death. Though the "thorn" may have persisted, Paul hung on fiercely to the truth, that God was faithful!

Beauty Instead of Ashes

Jacob also came to see that God was faithful and trustworthy when He finally brought him back to the land of his forefathers, just as He had promised (Genesis 31:3). Right before he entered the Promised Land, on the other side of the Jordan River, God met with him again. For many years Jacob had trusted in his own resources and his deceptive abilities to gain the upper hand with his father-in-law, Laban. Jacob had learned much, but not enough for him to enter the Promised Land as God had intended. Now on the brink of possibly losing all he had painstakingly accumulated – his two wives and two concubines, twelve children, numerous flocks and servants – he once again faced his brother Esau. Fear enveloped him, his mind spun scenarios of appeasement or escape. In the past, Jacob had brought all the previous difficulties on himself because of his choices. At those times, Jacob always had an escape route planned, just in case. But now God had him cornered and met with him, face to face. Engaging him in a wrestling match, God touched his hip and in crippling Jacob, finally taught him what it meant to lean on God. No longer confident in his strength or resources, Jacob now experienced how to fully trust his God. It had taken many years, much pain and disappointment, but God had perfected His man

Joseph languished for many years, forgotten and given up as dead before he was finally elevated to second in command of all the glories of Egypt. Imagine as he traced in his mind the journey he had taken, or rather that God had brought him through. His God had been

When God Deliberately Sends Trials

faithful, but his journey was not over. Joseph's last request was to bring his bones back to the Promised Land when the nation one day would leave Egypt. He knew he was not at home in Egypt, that one day Israel would return to the land that God had promised them. He saw this fulfillment as still in the future, yet by faith he was confident that even his dry bones would finally come to rest there. He lived out the remainder of his years in a foreign land, content to trust God's future plan that he could only see by faith. Joseph's faith was the same as his father's and grandfather's: tested, refined and grounded in God's trustworthy nature.

No one likes painful trials. No one chooses hard pillows. Rejection hurts and abandonment devastates. But God is there in the midst, speaking to you and to me. He desires to show us His plan, how even the trials are apportioned to us for our good and for His glory. It takes faith to step out of our comfort and trust Him in spite of how it looks. By faith we too can take our stone pillow and turn it upright. When we do, we will gain His perspective. We will see it as a place of worship, a place where we lay our lives, our plans, and our will on the altar. It is hard to let go of these, to pour oil on them, step back, and allow God to consume them. Just as the burning bush Moses encountered in the desert was not consumed, we will discover that our sacrifice will not consume us, but free us to more fully trust our God. He will be glorified in it and we will gain the peace that comes from trusting and depending on Him, no matter what the outcome or cost.

These men are examples to us of what it means to live for God, traveling through this land as a pilgrim and a stranger. These are the Patriarchs who saw the present realities, including suffering, as part of God's will. Together with them, God desires to perfect our faith in present sufferings in order to prepare us for an eternity with Him in heaven. Our inheritance and our reward are with Him in glory. Will you trust God as these men did? Take the stone and turn it. Take your trials, your suffering, your broken life and dreams; hold them up before God and turn them until you see them as an altar. See it from His perspective and stop your struggle. He has answered your prayers. Let Him teach you through each trial, what it means to trust Him. What you gain will be worth it.

Chapter Eight

When Heaven is Silent

And Jesus Does Not

Answer

My Son's Journey

Mary and Martha

King David

Mary, Jesus' Mother

*The Faithful
From
Hebrews 11*

When Heaven Is Silent and Jesus Does Not Answer

My Son's Journey

There are times as I minister to people who are struggling with God and crying out in pain, that it appears heaven is silent. It is hard to know exactly what to say. Sometimes I will share a verse from the Bible that sounds right and I hope will help. But I wonder if the person I am ministering to can tell that I am struggling, as they graciously thank me for my kind words, saying, "It really helped." I wonder though, if it did.

I have been in that lonely place, wrestling with God and receiving little response to my anguished cries. One example was when our son, Jamie, broke his leg in a skiing accident at the age of about eleven. It was his first time skiing. I had practically grown up skiing, so felt I would be the best one to introduce him to the sport. Not knowing if he would take to the sport, I borrowed boots from one friend and skis from another and up the mountain we went. Jamie was naturally athletic so he quickly picked up the basic techniques of the sport. Later that afternoon skiing down a rather icy slope, his ski tips crossed, sending him spiraling out of control. As I skied to his side I did not want to admit how seriously it looked. I sent up a hope and a prayer to God that this was nothing more than a sprain, but his desperate cries told me otherwise. He had indeed broken his leg.

At that moment I flashed back to my first time learning to ski. I was about his age. It was also a cold, icy day. I was learning to "snowplow," my skis forming a Vshaped wedge, easing me downhill under control. Somewhere out of nowhere, an evil root stuck its gnarly head up through the ice and caught my ski tip, sending me hurtling to a sure fall. Instinctively I put my hands forward to break my fall, but unfortunately my hands were still clutching my ski poles. One of those ski poles planted itself in the ice in the direct path of my face, which collided with it, bending it (the pole) to a 90-degree angle! Because of the icy conditions the first-aid toboggan was unable to take me down the hill. My sister slowly coaxed me down the hill where the medical staff examined my greatly swollen face. It is funny now, to recall my mom's reaction when she was summoned from the lodge. After conferring with the medical staff that I might have broken my nose and possibly incurred eye damage, she bent over my cot and exclaimed, "Susan, can you see me?" Struggling to peer through very swollen eyelids, I weakly responded, "Yes", to which she insisted, "You get up right now and go back up the mountain. I paid a lot for your ticket and I am not going to have you waste it lying in here all day." When my "junior high" emotions kicked in, I asked for a mirror. After all, I could not go out if I looked as badly as I felt, to which my mom emphatically declared, "Of course there are no mirrors here, this is a ski hill." Needles to say, I skied the rest of the day.

The day I took Jamie for his first ski venture, I remember praying for a better first time out than mine. It was against my better judgment that I had borrowed the

When Heaven Is Silent and Jesus Does Not Answer

ski equipment because it was not suited for him. Tragically it was the ill-fitting boot that failed to release from the ski that resulted in breaking his left leg - a spiral fracture of both the tibia and fibula. It was a heart wrenching experience for us both; he no doubt got the worst part, enduring a very painful recovery. My previous run-in with my ski pole left no lasting consequences. Not so for our son who suffered the unlikely scenario of eventual uneven leg growth. The injured leg did not keep pace with the other leg, slowly throwing his hips out of alignment. As his spine began to curve, a wedge was placed in his shoe to correct the imbalance. It was difficult to convince Jamie of the need for a special shoe and wedge in order to prevent long-term physical disabilities. Inwardly, I blamed myself for ignoring the warning bell in my mind. I had known better than to put anyone in borrowed equipment. How I wish I could go back in time, to spend the money to rent safe boots and skis that would have released when needed. But I cannot change the past.

Years later, another series of unfortunate decisions almost took our son's life. At the pinnacle of his life, his wedding a mere three weeks away, he survived a high-speed accident in the desert between Las Vegas and Los Angeles. The car in which he was riding rolled over many times. He was airlifted to a trauma center where we received the call that his life was spared. We counted our blessings that there were no head or spinal injuries. His arm, leg and heels however, were terribly lacerated when he had crawled through the broken window. These injuries were quickly minimized though. X-Rays revealed the chilling truth; each bone-jarring roll of the car had shattered his hips. Though it seemed the fractures were intact, the pain he suffered as he began therapy seemed out of proportion. After several weeks of unrelenting pain, the initial diagnosis was corrected. It seemed the fractures had indeed displaced and he was now healing with major shifts between the bones. Jamie underwent surgery to rebreak the bones and stabilize the hip fractures with pins, plates and screws. It was mind-numbing to see his X-rays, to see how they had pieced him together. But heal he did, as God's miraculous invention of the body slowly knit the bones back together. However, hidden to us but not to Jamie, there was another sensation that was different from the pain of the fractures. This was a strong, burning feeling of pins and needles coursing down his leg. The rollover trauma had not only fractured his hips but had also damaged the sciatic nerve that runs through the hips. This pain did not lessen with medication or time but persisted as a chronic and debilitating consequence of the accident. Fifteen months later, after massive drug therapy, physical therapy, and a host of alternative treatments that did not relieve his pain, surgery was scheduled to implant a device that would interrupt the pain signals from the foot to the brain. But that remedy was also interrupted by the doctor's "uh-oh" when he looked at Jamie's back. The remnants of his old ski accident - the curving of the spine and twisting of the hips due to uneven leg growth - put

When Heaven Is Silent and Jesus Does Not Answer

the success of surgery in grave doubt. For all of us, it was a gut-wrenching reminder that too often we must live with the consequences of our choices.

Jamie continues to search for a remedy to a life of chronic pain, to finally be able to piece back the life that was shattered by a series of unfortunate decisions. He is learning the sobering truth that consequences steal the joy from life and crush the spirit. "If only..." becomes the haunting question filling the mind. I wish a thousand times I could go back in time to change my thoughtless choice of ski equipment that has brought such suffering to my son. But I cannot. And I know my son has rehearsed in his mind the series of choices that led up to his accident. If he could, he would go back in time, listen to the small warning signs, and do things differently. But he cannot.

We are all human, frail, and often powerless. We cannot change the past but are left to deal with the present the best we can. So we pray, but sadly we often do not receive the answers we long for. It is then that we face choices: we can turn from God in bitterness, believing that He doesn't hear or care, or we can hold on in faith. Either way, there are no guarantees that we will see a miracle. Perhaps the miracle is to still trust God, believing that what He says is true. Faith helps me believe that one day Jamie will be whole and pain free.

There is a song, written by The Stoneleigh Band from Australia, called "There is a Day." The lyrics speak to situations like ours. They offer hope even when circumstances do not change and miracles do not happen. That hope is rooted in the truth of our eventual freedom from the pain and sorrow connected with this world, when one day we will step out of this life and into life eternal. Listen to these words of hope and future triumph. I pray that you will gain perspective for living through whatever you might be facing.

> *"There is a day*
> *That all creation's waiting for*
> *A day of freedom and liberation for the earth*
> *And on that day*
> *The Lord will come to meet His bride*
> *And when we see Him*
> *In an instant we'll be changed*
> *The trumpet sounds*
> *And the dead will then be raised*
> *By His power*
> *Never to perish again*
> *Once only flesh*
> *Now clothed with immortality*
> *Death has now been*
> *Swallowed up in victory*
> *We will meet Him in the air*
> *And then we will be like Him*
> *For we will see Him, as He is*
> *Oh yeah!*
> *Then all hurt and pain will cease*
> *And we'll be with Him forever*

When Heaven Is Silent and Jesus Does Not Answer

And in His Glory we will live
Oh yeah! Oh yeah!
So lift your eyes
To the things as yet unseen
That will remain now
For all eternity
Though trouble's hard
It's only momentary
And it's achieving
Our future glory."

(Reprinted by permission, Music Services, Inc.)

I am so glad the Bible was written under the inspiration of the Holy Spirit and therefore does not sugarcoat reality. It tells of real people who also struggled, were frustrated, and experienced disappointment. Some despaired of hope, faltered in faith, and stumbled into pits of depression. Their stories give me hope for my journey and for my son's. I want us to look at a few of these real flesh-and-blood people and listen as they share their experiences of how they endured when heaven was silent.

Mary and Martha

John 11:1-44

"Now a man named Lazarus was sick. He was from Bethany, the village of Mary and her sister Martha. This Mary, whose brother Lazarus now lay sick, was the same one who poured perfume on the Lord and wiped his feet with her hair. So the sisters sent word to Jesus, 'Lord, the

one you love is sick.'
When He heard this, Jesus said, 'This sickness will not end in death. No, it is for God's glory so that God's Son may be glorified through it.' Jesus loved Martha and her sister and Lazarus. Yet when He heard that Lazarus was sick, He stayed where He was two more days.
Then He said to His disciples, 'Let us go back to Judea.'
'But Rabbi,' they said, 'a short while ago the Jews tried to stone you, and yet you are going back there?'
Jesus answered, 'Are there not twelve hours of daylight? A man who walks by day will not stumble, for he sees by this world's light. It is when he walks by night that he stumbles, for he has no light.'
After He had said this, He went on to tell them, 'Our friend Lazarus has fallen asleep; but I am going there to wake him up.'
His disciples replied, 'Lord, if he sleeps, he will get better.' Jesus had been speaking of his death, but His disciples thought He meant natural sleep.
So then He told them plainly, 'Lazarus is dead, and for your sake I am glad I was not there, so that you may believe. But let us go to him.'
Then Thomas (called Didymus) said to the rest of the disciples, 'Let us also go, that we may die with him.'
On His arrival, Jesus found that Lazarus had already been in the tomb for four days. Bethany was less than two miles from Jerusalem, and many Jews had come to Martha and Mary to comfort them in the loss of their brother. When Martha heard that Jesus was coming, she went out to meet Him, but Mary stayed at home.

When Heaven Is Silent and Jesus Does Not Answer

'Lord,' Martha said to Jesus, 'if you had been here, my brother would not have died. But I know that even now God will give You whatever You ask.'
Jesus said to her, 'Your brother will rise again.'
Martha answered, 'I know he will rise again in the resurrection at the last day.'
Jesus said to her, 'I am the resurrection and the life. He who believes in Me will live, even though he dies; and whoever lives and believes in Me will never die. Do you believe this?'
'Yes, Lord,' she told Him, 'I believe that You are the Christ, the Son of God, who was to come into the world.' And after she had said this, she went back and called her sister Mary aside. 'The Teacher is here,' she said, 'and is asking for you.' When Mary heard this, she got up quickly and went to Him. Now Jesus had not yet entered the village, but was still at the place where Martha had met Him. When the Jews who had been with Mary in the house, comforting her, noticed how quickly she got up and went out, they followed her, supposing she was going to the tomb to mourn there.
When Mary reached the place where Jesus was and saw Him, she fell at his feet and said, 'Lord, if you had been here, my brother would not have died.'
When Jesus saw her weeping, and the Jews who had come along with her also weeping, He was deeply moved in spirit and troubled. 'Where have you laid him?' He asked.
'Come and see, Lord,' they replied.
Jesus wept.
Then the Jews said, 'See how He loved him!'

Beauty Instead of Ashes

But some of them said, 'Could not He who opened the eyes of the blind man have kept this man from dying?'
Jesus, once more deeply moved, came to the tomb. It was a cave with a stone laid across the entrance. 'Take away the stone,' He said.
'But Lord,' said Martha, the sister of the dead man, 'by this time there is a bad odor, for he has been there four days.'
Then Jesus said, 'Did I not tell you that if you believed, you would see the glory of God?'
So they took away the stone. Then Jesus looked up and said, 'Father, I thank You that You have heard Me. I knew that You always hear Me, but I said this for the benefit of the people standing here, that they may believe that You sent Me.'
When He had said this, Jesus called in a loud voice, 'Lazarus, come out!' The dead man came out, his hands and feet wrapped with strips of linen, and a cloth around his face.
Jesus said to them, 'Take off the grave clothes and let him go.'"

Many are familiar with the story of Jesus' friends, Mary, Martha and Lazarus. They were going about their normal everyday life when Lazarus got sick. He was one sick puppy! There were no antibiotics, no doctors with modern hospitals, X-ray machines, and MRIs. The only diagnosis was, "Call your friends, and make preparations, he is not going to make it through the night." It was a dreaded prognosis. Mary and Martha could not believe their ears as their walls were caving in. Desperately they clung to each other and sobbed. A glimmer of hope emerged as they whispered, "We will send for Jesus. He will come and heal our brother." Nodding in agreement and wiping their eyes on their sleeves, they must have gained hope and courage for themselves and for their brother. Perhaps it was something they remembered Jesus had said when He had shared a meal with them in their home (Luke 10:38-42). Mary had sat at His feet, spell-bound by His Words, which offered such peace, security, and comfort. Surely His Words would now be backed up by His actions.

Looking into their brother's bloodshot eyes and drawn face, they gathered their courage to confidently declare, "You will get well again; we will send word to Jesus! Hang in there brother, Jesus will come as soon as He hears of your sickness." With new found strength they quickly sent a servant to notify Jesus. Why, He was only in the next town and would receive word in a matter of hours. He would be there by nightfall, no later than tomorrow afternoon. Help was on the way.

But He did not come. Can you imagine their shock, their disbelief, their bitterness, and sense of betrayal? He most certainly had received the message. But, no Jesus. He did not come. Why? That bitter word, "Why", has echoed down through eternity with its pitiful cry from shattered hearts, broken dreams, and dashed hopes. How many emphatically declare they will line up, even if it takes all of eternity, to ask God, "Why did you let me down? Why didn't you do something? Why didn't you answer my prayer?"

Did Jesus show up for Mary and Martha? Eventually. Was He too late? At first it appeared He was. Yet His arrival was timed purposefully, to show them something He wanted them to know and to remember. Earlier He had given the disciples a forewarning of what He was planning, that this would be to the Father's glory and His. It seems He had already shared with His friends during an earlier visit to their home, for Martha knew of the resurrection at the last day. What she did not know was that He *was* the resurrection and the life! I believe Jesus was asking her to trust Him enough to allow this painful trial to reveal the glory of God and of His Son. "This sickness will not end in death" (11:4). Was this unfair, to require their pain and heartbreak in order to reveal God's glory? It is difficult to consider. Surely not for lack of love did Jesus allow them this pain and surely not because He was unaware of Lazarus' sickness and death. In fact it was their love for Him that was the basis for His asking. He was stretching them, showing them the extent of His power even over death. That power was manifested when He revealed Who He was – the Resurrection! It was for His glory but it was also for their good!

Possibly one of the cruelest verses in scripture is also the one that holds the greatest promise; "And we know that in all things God works for the good of those who love Him, who have been called according to His

When Heaven Is Silent and Jesus Does Not Answer

purpose" (Romans 8:28). Cruel when blurted out in the aftermath of tragedy, it rings hollow as a pious declaration that God somehow sees good in that which causes great anguish. How often this verse has sown bitter seeds in the hearts of people who experience loss, a cruel belief that God is so insensitive to their pain as to think it is good. So what does it mean?

"Now we see but a poor reflection as in a mirror; then we shall see face to face" (1 Corinthians 13:12). Much of our present day struggle with pain and sorrow exists because we don't see it the way God does; we lack the big picture perspective. Like the illustration of a tapestry, underneath it looks a mess, tangles and knots with no rhyme or reason. However when seen from above, suddenly it makes sense. You can see the pattern of a designer who fashions a masterpiece. Until we see God's purpose in pain, we will continue our desperate plea for why God allows suffering. So let's look at some scriptures that offer assurances to those who suffer and glimpses as to what lies ahead for those who persevere:

> *"After this I looked and there before me was a door standing open in heaven…*
> *At once I was in the Spirit, and there before me was a throne in heaven with Someone sitting on it…*
> *Surrounding the throne were twenty-four other thrones, and seated on them were twenty-four elders.*
> *They were dressed in white and had crowns of gold on their heads…*
> *Whenever the living creatures give glory, honor and*

> *thanks to Him who sits on the throne and who lives for ever and ever,*
>
> *the twenty-four elders fall down before Him who sits on the throne, and worship Him who lives for ever and ever. They lay their crowns before the throne and say:*
>
> *'You are worthy, our Lord and God, to receive glory and honor and power, for you created all things, and by Your will they were created and have their being.'"*
>
> Revelation 4:1-11 selected portions

Crowns in scripture represent the rewards given to those who obey God's will and live according to faith. This will happen at the end of time when there will be an accounting of believers, described in 2 Corinthians 5:10; "For we must all appear before the judgment seat of Christ, that each one may receive what is due him for the things done while in the body, whether good or bad." Listen to other passages that also refer to crowns and consider what scripture is telling us.

> *"Everyone who competes in the games goes into strict training. They do it to get a crown that will not last; but we do it to get a crown that will last forever."*
>
> I Corinthians 9:25
>
> *"Now there is in store for me the crown of righteousness, which the Lord, the righteous Judge, will award to me on that day – and not only to me, but also to all who have longed for His appearing."*   2 Timothy 4:8

When Heaven Is Silent and Jesus Does Not Answer

> *"Blessed is the man who perseveres under trial, because when he has stood the test, he will receive the crown of life that God has promised to those who love Him."*
>
> *James 1:12*
>
> *"And when the Chief Shepherd appears, you will receive the crown of glory that will never fade away."*
>
> *I Peter 5:4*
>
> *"I am coming soon. Hold on to what you have, so that no one will take your crown."*   *Revelation 3:11*

Crowns as rewards; could this be the reason and motivation for all who live for God, suffer, and even die for Him? There is more to life than just this life. There is an eternity that is determined by placing our faith in Jesus as Lord and Savior. The crowns we receive in heaven will be our reward, not only for obedience but also for perseverance. Once in heaven our only desire will be the incredible privilege to cast our crowns at His feet in praise of who He is and what He has done for us (Rev 4:11). Then, and only then, will we realize in the light of His glory that whatever we endured on this earth was worth it for Him. Only then will the aforementioned verse make sense; "In all things God works for the good of those who love Him."

That is why faith is so important. It enables us to walk in confidence, no matter what circumstances we face and to endure. Mary and Martha knew the Son of God intimately. They had shared dinner conversations, heard Him speak of His Father, and perhaps even the glories of heaven. When Lazarus became sick, Jesus delayed His coming to give them the profound experience of going from the depths of despair, when hope is lost, to the heights of splendor in seeing the reality of the resurrection. His question to them is the same to us; "Are you willing?" Mary and Martha might have hesitated till they saw in His eyes something familiar. Their friendship with Jesus was the basis for trust, even in the midst of that which appeared beyond hope. Trembling as if on the precipice of a cliff, not knowing what was going to happen, they led Jesus to the tomb. When Jesus commanded that the stone be rolled away, did they gasp in horror at what they perceived would be behind that stone? Did they visibly shudder when Jesus shouted for the dead to come forth? I believe they anticipated nothing short of a miracle as they stared at the opening of the grave. Lazarus did come forth, bound by the wrappings of the grave yet overcoming even the sting of death in the power of the resurrection!

Is this what Romans 8:28 means, "making all things good"? Before Jesus raised Lazarus from the dead, they were not able to see any good in his premature death. Yet I know Mary and Martha's faith resulted in crowns, which in heaven one day they would willingly and joyfully cast at the feet of Jesus. Soon after this miracle of resurrection, Mary would bend in love and gratitude to anoint Jesus' feet with costly oil and to dry them with her hair (John 12:1-3). Was she practicing what she considered her brother Lazarus had already done while briefly in heaven, casting crowns before the feet of Jesus? Is Jesus worth it? Can you trust Him?

King David

We leave Mary, Martha and Lazarus to travel back to the time of King David. David has much to tell us of his grievous suffering due to his sin, despite his confession and desperate appeals to God.

> *"In the spring, at the time when kings go off to war, David sent Joab out with the king's men and the whole Israelite army. But David remained in Jerusalem.*
> *One evening David got up from his bed and walked around on the roof of the palace. From the roof he saw a woman bathing. The woman was very beautiful, and David sent someone to find out about her. (She was the wife of Uriah, the Hittite) Then David sent messengers to get her. She came to him, and he slept with her. The woman conceived and sent word to David, saying, 'I am pregnant.'*
> *In the morning David wrote a letter to Joab...'Put Uriah in the front line where the fighting is fiercest.' When the men of the city came out and fought against Joab, some of the men fell; moreover, Uriah the Hittite was dead.*
> *When Uriah's wife heard that her husband was dead, she mourned for him. After the time of mourning was over, David had her brought to his house, and she became his wife and bore him a son. But the thing David had done displeased the Lord.*

Beauty Instead of Ashes

The Lord sent Nathan to David, who said to him, 'Why did you despise the word of the Lord by doing what is evil in His eyes?'

Then David said to Nathan, 'I have sinned against the Lord.'

Nathan replied, 'The Lord has taken away your sin. You are not going to die. But...the son born to you will die.'

David pleaded with God for the child. He fasted and spent the nights lying on the ground. On the seventh day the child died. Then David got up from the ground and went into the house of the Lord and worshiped. He answered, 'While the child was still alive, I fasted and wept. I thought, "Who knows? The Lord may be gracious to me and let the child live." But now that he is dead, why should I fast? Can I bring him back again? I will go to him, but he will not return to me.'

2 Samuel 11 and 12, selected verses

These events occurred during the golden era of the Kings of Israel, a noble and heroic time. King David was courageous, bold, dashing, handsome, and yes, clueless! What was he thinking, that he was too old to go off to war when springtime came? He most certainly was not, nor was he too old to fall for the oldest trick in the book, a beautiful woman in a very tempting situation. Bathsheba was enticing to an older man. David fell for the lure of a one-night stand and paid dearly for his mistake. David thought he had gotten away with deception, conspiracy and murder, but he forgot to look up. God was watching and through the prophet Nathan,

When Heaven Is Silent and Jesus Does Not Answer

informs David of the outcome. The grave misfortune that not only befell poor Uriah would also come to David and Bathsheba; the child born to Bathsheba would die. David spent not just one day in agony but a week on the ground. He begged, pleaded, and bargained with God to change the horrible consequence that one brief night of passion would inflict on his innocent child. Bathsheba's cries mingled with David's as she also wept and pleaded for the life of her son. But to no avail. Perhaps you can understand their lonely nights of desperation, when God seemed as far away as the twinkling stars set in a cold and empty sky. Not much was left to sustain their hope. God did not change His mind. The son Bathsheba bore to David died. Instead of throwing himself off the palace tower, which is what the servants feared, David picked himself up off the floor, washed, and allowed the servants to serve him food. For a whole week he had teetered on the edge of insanity over his son's impending death. Now that the child was dead, David composed himself. Why? Had he lost touch with reality? Was he so insensitive, perhaps because he had other sons? No, David had a father's heart and loved his new wife very much. But he also knew his God and realized that when life is in the balance, there is always hope. "Who knows? The Lord may be gracious to me and let the child live" (2 Samuel 12:22). But once death came, David knew his son would never come back to him but "he would go to the child" (12:23). David exhibited amazing understanding of the reality of life after death, which gives perspective and hope to those who weep and mourn. David and

Bathsheba held on to their belief that one day they would see their son, never to be separated again. Though sorrow would last for a time, it would dissolve with the morning sun. One day, they too, would experience what Paul would write much later on, "Death has been swallowed up in victory" (1 Corinthians 15:54).

Although there is not a lot of scripture regarding the eternal security of infants or of young children who die prematurely, these passages from 2 Samuel give profound hope to those who grieve deeply. Does God care? Was He there for David and Bathsheba? Yes, by giving them the confidence and strength to get up off the floor and to enter life again. The treasure they held, though not in their arms but in their hearts, was the assurance that they would see him again. It was enough.

Mary, Jesus' Mother

We continue our journey through scripture for an intimate look into the life of Mary, Jesus' mother. Few people have felt the heights of joy and the depths of sorrow like Mary. It is with awe and respect we allow scripture to reveal her story to gain perspective and hope for our journey.

> *"Near the cross of Jesus stood His mother. When Jesus saw His mother there, and the disciple whom He loved standing nearby, He said to His mother, 'Dear woman, here is your son,' and to the disciple, "here is your mother.'*

When Heaven Is Silent and Jesus Does Not Answer

"Later, knowing that all was now completed, and so that the Scripture would be fulfilled, Jesus said, 'I am thirsty.' When He had received the drink, Jesus said, 'It is finished.' With that, He bowed His head and gave up His spirit."
John 19:25-37 selected verses

Imagine with me, a wind-swept hill overlooking a lonely garden. A small group of women and men huddle together against the cold wind that had just kicked up, swirling the dry leaves about their feet. They look up through tear-filled eyes in disbelief at the still, broken bodies of three men hanging on cruel Roman crosses. They are dead now, their misery is over. Not so for those who are left behind. Mary bends over in grief, barely able to sustain herself. She had watched in horror as her Son had died before her eyes. "How could this be?" Her mind drifted back to a similar question she had breathed long ago as a mighty angel of the Lord had told her the amazing news of her future. She would become pregnant, even though a virgin. "How could this be?"

The angel Gabriel had given Mary assurance concerning the promise of the Messiah through a virgin (Isaiah 7:14). After His birth, Mary and Joseph brought their Child to the temple for dedication. There they received other affirmations through prophecy from Simeon, a righteous and devout man who was waiting for the consolation of Israel, and Anna, a prophetess. Simeon took the infant Jesus in his arms and praised God, saying, "My eyes have seen Your salvation...This Child is destined to cause the falling and rising of many

Beauty Instead of Ashes

in Israel…and a sword will pierce your own soul too" (Luke 2:25-35, selected verses).

Through the years of Jesus' public ministry, Mary had pondered these proclamations. At times she had experienced incredible delights as she witnessed prophecies come true. But there were also times when she had felt a sudden stab of pain, recalling Simeon's warning that a sword would also pierce her heart. And it had. Mary must have lurched in pain and horror as the soldiers' spear pierced Jesus' side as He hung defenseless on the rugged cross. As His heart had broken for the world, so too, her heart was broken, torn and shattered as she looked upon her Son, now dead. She had cried out to God to save His Son and hers. Even the voice of Jesus from the cross asked a haunting question, "Why have You forsaken Me?" How empty that cry as it dissipated into the wind and was swept away. Jesus hung His head and died. No answer was given to Him, not even to the Son of God. Poor, sweet Mary, now gently enfolded in the strong arms of John, slowly departed from the cross. Where was God? He was there. The Bible gives us clear understanding that this was the will of God, "to crush Him and cause Him to suffer" (Isaiah 53:10). Mary and the disciples had entered a very dark and lonely valley for three days, only to emerge into the bright light of resurrection morning!

When had they finally understood the words Jesus had spoken to them? He did prepare them for this. Perhaps in the excitement of His ministry they did not

When Heaven Is Silent and Jesus Does Not Answer

fully comprehend what He was talking about. But He had told them, He had prepared them, He had revealed to them the Father's plan and will. Mary certainly knew this was part of God's plan when Gabriel announced to her the coming birth of the Messiah. Simeon had predicted to Mary and Joseph both the joy and the woe of His advent. John the Baptist gave testimony of His purpose when he announced, "Look, the Lamb of God Who takes away the sin of the world" (John 1:29). In many of His teachings Jesus had referred to His life as fulfilling Old Testament scripture. But for the disciples and Mary, as they slowly left the bloodied cross, it seemed so long ago. Cradled deep within her mind where memory often fades, Mary probably recalled yet had wanted to forget His haunting Words:

> *"I am the Good Shepherd. The Good Shepherd lays down His life for the sheep."* John 10:11
>
> *"The hour has come for the Son of Man to be glorified. I tell you the truth, unless a kernel of wheat falls to the ground and dies, it remains only a single seed. But if it dies, it produces many seeds...it was for this very reason I came to this hour."* John 12:23-24, 27
>
> *"Do not let your hearts be troubled. Trust in God, trust also in Me. In my Father's house are many rooms; if it were not so, I would have told you. I am going there to prepare a place for you. And if I go and prepare a place for you, I will come back and take you to be with me that you also may be where I am."* John 14:1-3

Then, early on Sunday morning the mist of the unthinkable and the pain of the unimaginable gave way to joy as Mary and the disciples experienced firsthand the fulfillment of prophesy. Every one of His Words came true when He stood in their midst to proclaim He was alive! Mary and the disciples had Jesus with them another forty wonderful days before He left them again. It must have been very hard to see Him ascend into heaven in a cloud. How long they waited there, watching and longing for His return, we don't know. An angel finally told them to stop looking for His return and get busy obeying His will (Acts 1:11). The disciples departed, eagerly discussing among themselves the thoughts and plans that were forming in their hearts, the excitement mounting as they realized the task Jesus had commissioned them for. But Mary slowly walked away from the hill where she had last seen her Son. I believe she smiled, for she knew she would see Him again. Faith had brought her through this far. She knew God would see her through her own death, which would be her entrance into life eternal. She knew that was where she would see Jesus.

The Faithful from Hebrews 11

We finish with a brief look into one of the most compelling chapters of the Bible. Hebrews 11 is referred to as the "chapter of faith." It reads like a "Who's Who," listing the giants from biblical times. Beginning at creation and Abel's sacrifice, it mentions Enoch, who did not experience death; Noah, who built the ark; and Abraham, the father of the faithful. It said that though they lived by faith, "they did not receive the things promised" (Hebrews 11:13). Others mentioned are Isaac, Jacob, Joseph and Moses. Lesser-known personalities are then briefly listed before the chapter finishes by describing two groups of people: those who received what was promised and those who did not. Read what "those who received" experienced, in verses 33-35:

> *"Who through faith conquered kingdoms, administered justice, and gained what was promised; who shut the mouths of lions, quenched the fury of the flames, and escaped the edge of the sword; whose weakness was turned to strength; and who became powerful in battle and routed foreign armies. Women received back their dead, raised to life again."*

If we stopped there, we would observe that God had given these people extraordinary faith to go through what they did and to triumph. We might conclude that this is the legacy of all who believe and live by faith. Yet when we read the following verses, 35b-39, we are startled to see what "those who did not receive" experienced. It was quite different from the first group.

> *"Others were tortured and refused to be released, so that they might gain a better resurrection. Some faced jeers and flogging, while still others were chained and put in prison. They were stoned; they were sawed in two; they were put*

> *to death by the sword. They went about in sheepskins and goatskins, destitute, persecuted and mistreated – the world was not worthy of them. They wandered in deserts and mountains, and in caves and holes in the ground. These were all commended for their faith, yet none of them received what had been promised."*

Why the discrepancy between these two groups? No answer is given. Surely it was not that some were worthy or more deserving, for the author defended those who suffered as those of whom "the world was not worthy" (11:38a).

What do we make of this? Simply this, that in this life there will be pain, some will suffer greatly, and others will be victorious. Where is the justice? As the author of Hebrews goes on to explain, our focus in life is not in the here and now. It is in heaven where someday we will find our rest, our comfort, and our reward. Unless we let go of our belief that this is our final destiny and reward, we will never experience the true reward of faith. The author of Hebrews intended to communicate what the people of faith had learned through their journey, including both the triumphs and defeats. We read of their discovery, in verses 13-16:

> *"All these people were still living by faith when they died, they did not receive the things promised; they only saw them and welcomed them from a distance. And they admitted that they were aliens and strangers on earth. People who say such things show that they are looking for*

> *a country of their own...they were longing for a better country – a heavenly one."*

It was this perspective in life that enabled those of faith to hold on to what they could not see and to hold on resolutely. Dimly they perceived a world not yet their own, which was worth the journey and worth the cost. With confident courage and unwavering commitment they lived bold and daring lives, faced their tormentors and slayers, and entered heaven triumphant. "Therefore God is not ashamed to be called their God, for He has prepared a city for them" (11:16). Apparently this was enough for them.

The Apostle Paul also refers to this perspective when he writes in 2 Corinthians 5:1, 4:

> *"For we know that if our earthly house, this tent, is destroyed, we have a building from God, a house not made with hands, eternal in the heavens. ...For we who are in this tent groan, being burdened, not because we want to be unclothed, but further clothed, that mortality may be swallowed up by life."*

And in 1 Corinthians 15:54, Paul says:

> *"When the perishable has been clothed with the imperishable, and the mortal with immortality, then the saying that is written will come true: 'Death has been swallowed up in victory.'"*

Paul believed this, which enabled him to fearlessly face his tormentors and to endure the death of a martyr.

Beauty Instead of Ashes

He was so convinced of this perspective on life and death that he actually struggled with the desire to go to be with Jesus, which he said was far better than staying on earth! Yet he also knew it was God's will for him to linger for other's sake and so he was content to remain (Philippians 1:21-25).

What have we learned through the lives of these biblical people? They are really no different from you and me. Like Mary and Martha, King David, and Mary, Jesus' mother, no one likes pain and suffering. No one cherishes final goodbyes. There is sadness and an ache that comes to a heart when the one who is loved is torn away. When heartbreak happens we cry out for relief. Though God does not always give us what we want, I believe He gives us what we need, which is Himself. Some call it "delayed gratification," the ability to put off what we want now in order to receive something better later on. Much of our struggle and desire on earth is that we want to experience the reality of heaven here. We need to remember that our life on earth is not our final destination; we will not live here forever. Not until death takes us out of this temporary existence and into eternity will we experience the joys of perfection. Not until then will we see Jesus face to face. So, until that time, we must be content with what He gives us now, His Holy Spirit. Is that enough? It should be. A lot depends on how we view this life and the life to come, which is heaven.

Mary and Martha believed that Jesus was the resurrection and life, and they rejoiced!

When Heaven Is Silent and Jesus Does Not Answer

David embraced the future eternal life that he and his son would one day enjoy together, and found strength.

Mary, Jesus' mother, trusted His words about the heavenly home He was going to prepare for her, and was comforted.

The heroes of faith believed the God of the Old Testament who promised an inheritance that would never be taken from them. They were victorious, in life and in death!

I found a saying I had written in my Bible, which has given me perspective for the trials of life.

> *"There is a peace that comes after sorrow, in hope surrendered, not in hope fulfilled."*
>
> *Author Unknown*

This speaks of letting go, not into despair, but into the arms of the One who will never abandon me. "Underneath are the everlasting arms" (Deuteronomy 33:27), and it is into those arms I know I can trust my loved ones and myself. Is peace what you are after, what you seek because of sorrow? This can be yours as you place your faith and trust in the One who will never let you go.

I hope to be like Mary and Martha who said in the face of death, "I know he will rise again." Or like David who looked forward to seeing his son at his own death. Or like Mary who no doubt embraced her Son with relish but also let Him go into glory. She knew she would see Him again. What confidence, what victory!

What about our son and his journey through this trial of pain and consequences? It is still ongoing. It is his "waiting room," as at times it is as threatening as "the valley of the shadow of death" (Psalm 23:4). That shadow at times seems so real. His faith is strong, he holds on with a resilience I have never seen before; he has never been tested like this before. I find it easier to also hold on to faith when I see it so clearly in him. What I also know is that one day Jamie will be whole and healed, his back straight, legs even, perhaps even the scars on his body will disappear. How do I know this? Jesus showed it by rising from the dead. His broken body was transformed into a glorified body, free from that which had cruelly marred and killed Him. Though Jesus still retains His scars, reminders of His love and what it cost Him, His resurrection body is the model of what we have to look forward to, and I do so with utmost hope.

I also believe God's heart breaks when He sees sin and the consequences of choices and decisions that devastate so many lives. I believe He cries with us as Jesus did at the grave of Lazarus, wrestling with His emotions of love, loss and anger toward death. I believe His healing of some and not others is to teach us not to look for life's fulfillment here and now. Our focus can be so narrow, only looking at our present circumstances and not to the fullness of all that He has prepared for us. We need to see that a temporary healing now is but a foretaste, a glimpse of what He longs to give us in full when we see Him face to face.

While we wait for that wonderful day when we will receive our glorified bodies, God wants us to trust Him now. You cannot trust someone you do not know. This then, is His will; that when we truly know Him, we will be able to trust Him fully to allow suffering and pain to transform us into His likeness. What will that likeness look like? Like Jesus, Whose life showed such patience, humility, gentleness, and compassion. As God "perfected" His Son Jesus through what He suffered (Hebrews 2:10), is this not also His way with us? Should we be surprised at His pathway? If it was good enough for Jesus, it should not be beneath us. But that takes perspective, the willingness and ability as Jacob discovered to "turn the stone" in order to see it from God's view. Then we can "give thanks in all circumstances, for this is God's will for you in Christ Jesus" (1 Thessalonians 5:18).

Where is God when you hurt? Does Jesus care? I hope I have answered these questions, maybe not as fully as you wanted but enough for faith to take over. It is a walk of faith, a journey we are on. Let's walk in confidence of the One who called us to Himself.

We leave this portion of the book for a look into my own journey. I pondered if I should include my story. I decided I would, in the hopes that it may encourage others who struggle with fear and with doubt. What I

Beauty Instead of Ashes

have experienced through the trials and tests of my life is God's unending patience, love and grace. Looking back I am overwhelmed by His touch on my life and I want this to be a tribute to His glory! I do so humbly, with the hope that it may also touch your life and encourage you to never give up, always look up, and be strengthened in your faith.

Part 3

Personal Reflections

Chapter Nine

Correctly Detached, Properly Aligned

Correctly Attached, Properly Aligned

The Bible is filled with wonderful stories of faith, courage, and heroism, designed by God to impact our lives. These stories bring us closer to God and give understanding regarding our own lives. One story from the Old Testament changed my life completely. It happened a few years ago when I was going through a time of confusion and depression. God graciously showed me how my life ran parallel with that of Abram, which revealed the error of my thinking and my behavior. Nobody likes difficulties, but it is what God often uses to reveal truth. My story is how God loved me so much that He would not allow me to continue in my error.

My story begins when my husband, Greg, graduated from seminary and we took a small, fledgling church outside Hartford, Connecticut. With a baby in tow and hopes for several more, we were idealistic and excited. We "cut our teeth" with a handful of sweet, lovely Christians with whom we quickly developed strong friendships and together launched ministries. We witnessed God's gracious hand in many miraculous ways. My best friends were women my own age. We had much in common as God added precious babies to our families at about the same time. Hence we shared everything: the joys and woes of child-rearing, marriages and church life. Not a day went by that I was not on the phone or meeting my friends to talk, share, or watch each other's children. We also developed close ties through Bible study and prayer, entering deeply into one another's lives. We learned crafts together: stenciling, quilting, and woodworking, anything that enabled us to have a sense of accomplishment. We delighted to be able to say at the end of the day, "Look what I did" and show something tangible in hand. A vivid and humorous memory was the day we wove baskets in my kitchen. Sitting cross-legged on the floor we wove baskets using reeds, which were soaking in big tubs on the floor. They say weaving is mindless work, but it was the best therapy to make a lovely basket all by myself.

My family heritage, which dates back to 1741 was nearby, nestled in the rolling hills south of Hartford, in Middlefield, Connecticut. One of the largest family run farms in the area, it boasts picturesque orchards and challenging golf courses. My grandparents were still living when we were in Connecticut. Each week I would visit them, relishing the down-home comfort of sipping coffee in Grandma's farm kitchen. I was so content and secure being close to my family heritage.

However, I did not realize that my emotional roots were going deeply into the soil of New England and my spiritual roots were enmeshed there as well. In my heart I was so content, I wanted nothing more than to live and to die there. My needs were fully met: I had a loving husband, a growing church ministry, family nearby, and friends that were worth their weight in gold. But God's plans conflicted with my plans. I was living out of His will and so began His loving correction.

Correctly Attached, Properly Aligned

In our seventh year of ministry in Connecticut, Greg shared with me his growing conviction that God was preparing to move us. He believed that for our good and the church's good, it was time we looked for a new church. My mind did not comprehend what he was saying. It was as if he was speaking another language. Move? Why? I was happy. I was content. I did not hear what he was saying nor believe it because I was so happy. Do you see the problem here? In my desperate attempt to cling to what I knew and what I loved, I was ignoring the fact that God was speaking through my husband. It was God who was asking us to move. My feelings, however, prevented me from recognizing God's voice and I remained resolute in my determination to stay put.

Greg had learned many things as a pastor those first seven years. He learned that a pastor is most effective when correctly detached from the task in order to better understand, respond, and lead. The operative word is "correctly," for the leader is not to be distant, unsympathetic, uncaring or calloused, but involved in such a way that he is available yet objective. Greg preached about this principle of "correct detachment" by expounding on Abram's call from God to leave Ur and travel to a land He would show him.

> *"The Lord had said to Abram, 'Leave your country, your people and your father's household and go to the land I will show you. I will make you into a great nation and I will bless you; I will make your name great, and you will*

> *be a blessing. I will bless those who bless you, and whoever curses you I will curse; and all peoples on earth will be blessed through you."* Genesis 12:1-3

What God had called Abram to leave in Ur was his name (family), his place (country), and his security (his father's household). What God promised him in return was a name (great nation), a place (the Promised Land), and security ("I will bless those who bless you, and curse those who curse you"). God was asking the same of us: to leave our name (family), our place (Connecticut), and our security (friends and family), and go to the place He would show us. He was asking me to trust Him enough to be correctly detached from these things so that I could be of use for Him. The writer of Hebrews spoke in a similar way to encourage believers in their walk of faith. He realized they also struggled with becoming attached and enamored with the things of this world; "Let us throw off everything that hinders and the sin that so easily entangles, and let us run with perseverance the race marked out for us. Let us fix our eyes on Jesus…" (12:1-2). Jesus also spoke about the need for detachment; "If anyone would come after Me, he must deny himself and take up his cross daily and follow Me" (Luke 9:23). Greg had learned this important principle as he encountered many situations that required him to be objective, conviction-driven, correctly detached and yet caring. Apparently, I had not learned the same lesson.

Right about that time a church in the south extended a call for Greg to become their pastor. We flew there one weekend to begin an initial candidating process. Everything about the church was "right" and I could not deny the call to go there was apparent. But I was not ready to say "good-bye" to our church in Connecticut. Oh, how deeply those roots had grown! Greg was so convinced of the need for us to be in full agreement and because we were not, he very kindly declined their offer. We flew home in silence. I was relieved that was over and could get back to what I was doing, serving the Lord in Connecticut! A year went by. Another call came from the same church. This time they were in desperate need. Again we flew there for a weekend to talk. Again, I could not deny the fact that everything seemed to be pointing to this being the Lord's will, except my heart. I was still not ready; my roots were still too deeply entrenched. Not being in agreement, Greg again declined their offer. We flew home again, in silence.

Things were different at home this time. There was not the same sense of purpose, mission, and belonging. Peace was not there. Something was wrong. My eyes were beginning to open to the truth. God had called us to leave, follow, and obey. Greg was willing but I was not. It was very painful to finally realize that I had rebelled against the Lord by following my will, my purpose, and my design for my life. Though Greg assured me that God's sovereignty was in control and that this was part of His plan, I realized my sin. I had allowed my roots to penetrate deeply into the soil of New England and not into His kingdom. I was not detached from the land, church, and family in order to obey His call to go to the land, church, and family of His choosing. In direct defiance of Him I had served myself in ministry and this I believe had terrible consequences on our church and the church in the South. In anguish I cried out to God for forgiveness and cleansing, which He mercifully granted. Through restoration I promised I would never again let my roots go deeply into any soil. I resolved I would be free from entanglements in order to obey His call, no matter when it might come or where it might lead. And I began the painful process of saying goodbye to the land of my birth, to my family and to my friends. Those farewells tore my heart like tender roots being torn from the soil. I was finally experiencing what it meant to be correctly detached.

Returning to Abram's story, we see that he obeyed and left everything behind. Although there was an apparent delay in Haran (Genesis 11:31), he finally arrived in the Promised Land of Canaan (12:4-5). I do not read of any reaction on Abram's part: no crying, no tears, and no farewell parties. At least I had a farewell party with my friends, where for the first time I heard the amazing song by Michael W. Smith, "Friends are Friends Forever". Talk about tears – we flooded the place with tears from that song.

> *"Friends are friends forever, if the Lord's the Lord of all… Though it's hard to let you go, in the Father's hand we know, that a lifetime's not too long, to live as friends".*

Correctly Attached, Properly Aligned

Still to this day, whenever I hear that song I am flooded with memories of my friends in Connecticut. It is also mixed with sorrow over my sin, its consequences, and its scars on my heart.

We moved to Wisconsin in the fall of 1986, settling into a lovely neighborhood and ministering in our new congregation. We had lived nine wonderful years in Connecticut. I was sure our time in Wisconsin would be brief and I had wondered if we might someday return to Connecticut. I doubted it would ever happen and tried not to let myself ponder it. I had resolved to learn my lesson; I would never again allow my roots to sink into any soil. I knew I could never go through the painful process of leaving another "Connecticut," and so the years began to fly by. I thought it was odd that I did not make intimate friends in Wisconsin as I had in Connecticut. But after all, I reasoned, I had promised God and myself that I would never again become so entrenched in any place nor so dependent on friends for my happiness. I also knew God was holding me to my promise to remain open to His call and to obey Him. We were now in the "Promised Land" and I was going to keep my roots shallow. So, with joy and a sense of God's blessing, I dove into ministry in our new church home. In no time I was teaching women's Bible studies in our church, in the inner city, and in our neighborhood. I was involved in Christian Education, made lots of new church friends, volunteered at our children's schools, and was active in a local philanthropic organization that raised funds for women's education. My days were busy and full of satisfaction and contentment - I was happy again! I loved being a pastor's wife. It was the most wonderful, meaningful, and fulfilling role I could ever have imagined. Greg was a wonderful husband and pastor who zealously guarded our family life but who also "greased the skids for me to fly" in ministry. And fly I did, till it all came crashing to earth.

In both of the churches we served, Greg and I experienced a growing conviction to include missions at the heart of everything we did. Not surprisingly, more and more opportunities opened for Greg to travel and to teach. But each time he returned, I could see the change in his heart. God was slowly but very visibly changing his heart, from serving the local church to ministering in the world. God had captured His man. After only four and one half years of a very fruitful and dynamic ministry, Greg offered his resignation and entered the world of being a global traveler. It is sad and difficult for a pastor to leave a church but not to leave the area. We learned this first hand. We left the church in which we had poured our lives over the previous years and attended a church nearby. On occasion Greg was invited to preach at this new church and so he maintained an involvement in the local ministry. And as usual I was seated in the congregation with our children, either listening intently to Greg preach or when he was traveling, to the senior minister, Pastor Marc. But I had lost my identity as the pastor's wife and in this new church I was pretty much unknown. I did chuckle a few times when those seated nearby warmly greeted me, obviously showing tenderness and compassion to what appeared to be a single mom with three adolescent children. I was proud of that church and the way they treated me. But I found my connection there was not enough, I needed more. I had not discovered a ministry within the church to get involved in, a niche in which to bloom. Strange feelings of depression were beginning to make inroads into my mind and heart, feelings I could not shake. In desperation, not knowing what to do or where to find myself, I enrolled at a seminary in Illinois across the border from Wisconsin. I commuted twice a week, navigating 75 miles of traffic each way into the suburbs north of Chicago. I threw myself into my studies with relish and abandon; I had finally found a purpose and a goal. It took a while for my mind to "wake up" again, but a few months of endless reading and studying did the trick. Those years flew by as I studied under gifted Christian professors, engaged in lively debate with fellow students, wrote papers, devoured books, and finally graduated in the spring of 1996, magna cum laude! But those feelings of depression snuck up on me again and I was feeling lost, without a purpose, and without meaning. My graduation day, instead of being the beginning of a bright new future, marked the beginning of a dark tunnel of depression. I had grown up in a loving Christian family, so the idea of a Christian in depression did not fit. I was ashamed of the way I was feeling. After all, I had everything a person could want in order to be happy: a loving family and a husband who adored me and did everything he could to make me happy. Many times I would cry in frustration and try to hide my tears from others. It was also very hard for Greg to see me and not be able to help. Life doesn't always go the way you want or the way you planned.

We started attending yet another church where I was able to use my degree in Christian Education. That brought back joy and meaning, for a while. As I fell back into familiar territory of teaching women's Bible studies, God providentially led me to teach the book of Genesis. That's when God opened my eyes to the continuing story of Abram.

> *"So Abram left, as the Lord had told him (12:4)...and they set out for the land of Canaan, and they arrived there" (12:5).*

Suddenly I was seeing something I had not seen before. I had more in common with Abram than I realized. Like Abram, God had called me to leave something very precious, something I thought I could not do without. While still in Connecticut I had learned to let go of my attachments to place, family, and friends, those things that had met my needs for security and comfort. I now held onto God very tightly, for He promised to meet those needs. I was now "correctly detached." As Abram left his attachments and followed God's leading, so I saw I had left my attachments and was now in a new place. But as I continued to study Genesis I came upon other passages through which God was teaching me yet another lesson.

> *"Abram traveled through the land...he built an altar there to the Lord who had appeared to him (12: 6, 8). From there he went on toward the hills east of Bethel...and built an altar (12:8). Now there was a famine in the land, and Abram went down to Egypt to live there for a while because the famine was severe (12:10). From the Negev he went from place to place until he came to Bethel, to the place...where his tent had been earlier and where he had first built an altar. There Abram called on the name of the Lord."*
> *Genesis 13:3-4*

Repetition in scripture tells us to look for something important. One might have expected Abram to believe that this new land would provide wonderful blessings of a new location to build security, find happiness and contentment. But instead I noticed that Abram traveled through the Promised Land building altars wherever he went. It appeared the more he traveled, the more he discovered that even the Promised Land disappoints. God had declared to Abram that the land was his, but in reality he did not own even a grain of sand. As he journeyed he also noticed that he was the alien, a stranger in a foreign land. It wasn't long before he experienced a major famine and resorted to a hasty retreat to Egypt. Notice that when he came back to Bethel he built an altar there (13:3-4). In his search for the true meaning of the "Promised Land," he returned to find it at Bethel. "Bethel" means "house of God." In Abram's journey throughout the land he discovered what God had intended to teach him; it does not matter where you go or what you do, as long as you remember to Whom you belong. He had finally learned his lesson. Abram's altars became his act of worship. As he piled stone upon stone, his gaze looked upward toward heaven and away from the things of the land. Then he placed his sacrifice on the fire. Still looking up, his arms now empty because the sacrifice had been placed, he worshipped God. He was now properly aligned. His focus was where it needed to be, on God and nothing else. Abram learned the secret of contentment; it is not where you are, what you have, or what you do. Contentment is found in God and your act of worship reveals that you are properly aligned with God. Only then did Abram receive from God the assurance that generations would come from him and that they would inherit the Promised Land. Abram learned to let go of what was promised in order to hold onto Who was his true inheritance. He continued to live in the land as a stranger and pilgrim, owning nothing but being content. Abram was properly aligned. It did not matter to him what he had or did not have. He had God and that was enough.

Through teaching His Word, God opened my eyes to see more clearly the error of my way. Previously in Connecticut, I had been incorrectly attached to name, place and security. I had learned through great pain to be correctly detached from everything but God. Now in Wisconsin, I was beginning to see that I had also been improperly aligned, and of all things, to ministry! I thought I had learned the biggest lesson in Connecticut by cutting the cords that bound me to anything but Him. What I had done in Wisconsin was become so attached and aligned to ministry that it had become my "god." I had drawn my purpose, my joy, and my contentment from my involvement in ministry and not from God. God loved me too much to allow this to continue. He is a "jealous God" and would not share my love with another (Exodus 34:14). God took my ministry involvement away, but He did this for my good to show me what I had done. Suddenly the source of my depression became clear. I was mourning the loss of involvement. I was lost without my connection to ministry. It was painful to realize I had substituted ministry for God. I needed to repent, to let go of any need to be important or useful. I also needed to let go of my identity as a pastor's wife or as a Christian Education director, or any other role I had in ministry. As I let go of those things, I clung fiercely to God and I could feel His arms holding tightly onto me. It felt so good! I was finally discovering my true identity, being *in Christ*, and I fell in love with Him. A new hunger awakened in me as I eagerly read through the Gospel accounts of Jesus' life. I discovered the security, peace and fulfillment I was longing for in knowing who I was. I was His child and that was enough for me.

Correctly detached and properly aligned. Abram's life exhibited the need to learn these important principles, as does mine. This phrase, *correctly detached and properly aligned,* has become a valuable tool for me to measure and evaluate my mind and my heart. Am I *correctly detached* from people and places and attached only to God? Are my roots shallow enough so that if God called me to another place, would I be willing to go? I believe you only have to experience the pain of your emotional roots being torn from the ground once, to know you never want to experience that again. It is not that I love my family any less but I know that to hold on to them, instead of obeying God, would not bring the contentment I desire. I would also forfeit the greater joy of being in God's will. Am I *properly aligned* to God, allowing my needs of security and significance to be met fully by God? This is a lesson I am still learning. God made me task-oriented and motivationally driven, which keeps me very busy and involved in ministry. Hence, I realize my need to check my heart often, to make sure my drive for ministry is in its proper balance. It would be very easy for me to slip into the trap of gaining a sense of value, importance, or significance from ministry. The only way to prevent this is to stay very much in love with Jesus. That way, if all my ministry involvement was to one day disappear, I would still be secure in my connection with Him. He is, and must be, my reason for living and for ministering, for He is the One who gives me worth and security. To be *properly aligned* is to worship God. It begins with admitting my emptiness apart from Him. I then recognize His holiness and all that He desires to pour into me, which is what I really needed all along. As I kneel before Him, He lovingly reaches to hold me,

Correctly Attached, Properly Aligned

giving me a sense of completeness and satisfaction. As I worship Him, He gives me Himself. He will not accept less for He desires to give me what is best. To look to anyone or anything else to meet my needs, which would take the place of God, would be foolish. Lord willing, I will not allow that to ever happen again!

Abram's journey was not over, nor is mine. There are more lessons to learn and more tests of faith in which God will show Himself to be faithful and sufficient.

Where is God when you hurt? Does He turn His back when disaster strikes? Though that may seem to be true, do not believe it. God is near and He does care. He has sent Jesus to show you His love, to encourage you in the trial, and to remind you of your heavenly inheritance. Too often we make the mistake to think that our life here on earth is all there is. It is one of the biggest deceptions of Satan, which can be devastating when our hopes and dreams are dashed. God knows how sin ruins everything and He understands when we suffer. That is why He promises heaven to His children, to those who know Him through personal faith. Heaven is where all our hopes and dreams will come true and where He will wipe away every tear. Our life is brief here on earth and for many it can be very painful and disappointing. But in heaven there will be an eternity of joy, bright sunshine, and rich and meaningful fellowship among brothers and sisters of faith. Faith is the ability to see beyond the pain of today to the bright hope of tomorrow and to wait for it patiently. I trust this book has helped you in your

Beauty Instead of Ashes

journey. My prayer is that you have gained new insights, a clearer perspective on suffering and pain, and received encouragement through the life of Jesus. It has been a blessing to write as God has reminded me of many things and has shown me more things I need to learn as well. The truth I hold onto, more than anything else, is that in Jesus, He has given me *beauty instead of ashes*. I know He wants to do the same for you!

ISBN 1425127479